Most Memorable Meals

Old-Fashioned Meals Have Stood the Test of Time

GOOD TASTE never goes out of style—the old-fashioned meals in this cookbook deliciously prove it! In fact, your own family will be just as eager to gather around the table for classic comfort food as you were when your mother—or grandmother—served it.

Most Memorable Meals contains 48 complete menus showcasing simple yet satisfying dishes like those you grew up with. The 192 cherished recipes found inside come from fellow cooks from across the country, who were pleased to pass on their family's favorites.

The mouth-watering main dishes, sides, breads and desserts call for everyday ingredients, include easy-to-follow directions and have been tested by our *Taste of Home* Test Kitchen staff. Best of all, we've included a full-color photo of *every single meal* so you can see what the dishes will look like before you start cooking. You can make these down-home meals for your clan with complete confidence!

This cookbook is sure to hold a valued place in your collection— it contains something for every season and appetite, plus, you can mix and match the 192 recipes with favorites from your own files for countless more menus.

So why not reach for *Most Memorable Meals* and head to the kitchen? Then sit down to a family dinner that won't be forgotten anytime soon!

Most Memorable Meals

Spring Meals...4

Summer Meals...30

Fall Meals...56

Winter Meals...82

Index...108

Editor: Jean Steiner
Art Director: Judy Larson
Food Editor: Janaan Cunningham
Associate Food Editors: Coleen Martin, Diane Werner
Senior Recipe Editor: Sue A. Jurack
Recipe Editor: Janet Briggs
Associate Editors: Heidi Reuter Lloyd, Susan Uphill
Food Photography: Rob Hagen, Dan Roberts
Senior Food Photography Artist: Stephanie Marchese
Food Photography Artist: Julie Ferron
Photo Studio Manager: Anne Schimmel
Graphic Art Associates: Ellen Lloyd, Catherine Fletcher
Chairman and Founder: Roy Reiman
President: Russell Denson

©2004 Reiman Media Group, Inc.
5400 S. 60th St., Greendale WI 53129
International Standard Book Number: 0-89821-385-1
Library of Congress Control Number: 2003096314
All rights reserved.
Printed in U.S.A.

pp. 10-11

pp. 20-2

pp. 12-13

pp. 14-15

Spring Meals

Mustard-Glazed Ham • Creamy Asparagus Casserole • Potato Rolls • Spring Fruit Salad 7

Braised Beef Rolls • Cream of Mushroom Soup • Special Brussels Sprouts • George Washington Cherry Cobbler..........................9

Butter Roast Chicken • Asparagus Supreme • Cool Cucumber Salad • Pineapple Cheesecake Squares.....................................11

Corned Beef and Cabbage • Irish Soda Bread • Beet Relish • Emerald Isle Cake 13

Ham Cups with Cherry Sauce • Macaroni Au Gratin • Orange Buttermilk Salad • Rhubarb Peach Shortcake 15

Broiled Fish • Roasted New Potatoes • Blue Cheese Salad • Baked Lemon Pudding...17

Tasty Sloppy Joes • Cheddar Mushroom Macaroni • Basil Dill Coleslaw • White Chocolate Chip Hazelnut Cookies................19

Pork Roast with Spiced Apples • Sweet-and-Sour Green Beans • Spoon Rolls • Bananas 'n' Cream Bundt Cake 21

Ham 'n' Egg Casserole • Blue-Ribbon Doughnuts • Old-World Puff Pancake • Creamy Fruit Bowl 23

Leg of Lamb • Mixed Greens Salad • Mother's Manicotti • Easter Pie.....................25

Deep-Dish Chicken Potpie • Ginger Pear Gelatin • Fruit Cooler • Orange Chiffon Cake 27

Steak Over Potatoes • Buttery Carrots 'n' Onions • Salad with Tomato-Green Pepper Dressing • Crisp Lemon Sugar Cookies........29

Mustard-Glazed Ham

My mom was known as the best cook in the county. This delicious glaze was in her collection of handwritten recipes. I laminated the ones I use most often, and this favorite was included. It's easy to prepare, and everyone seems to like ham made this way.   —Dorothy Smith El Dorado, Arkansas

1 fully cooked boneless ham (4 to 5 pounds)
3/4 to 1 cup water
1/4 cup orange marmalade
1/4 cup prepared mustard
1/4 teaspoon ground ginger

Place ham in a shallow roasting pan; add water to pan. Bake, uncovered, at 325° for 1 hour. In a bowl, combine marmalade, mustard and ginger; mix well. Brush some over the ham. Bake 1 hour longer or until a meat thermometer reads 140°, brushing occasionally with glaze. **Yield:** 12-15 servings.

Creamy Asparagus Casserole

My sister created this recipe and shared it with me. I always serve it on special holidays, particularly Easter. My husband says he hates asparagus, but he loves this casserole. He doesn't know he's eating his "enemy vegetable"!   —Joyce Allison, Millsap, Texas

2 pounds fresh asparagus, cut into 1-inch
**   pieces**
1/4 cup butter *or* margarine
1/4 cup all-purpose flour
2 cups milk *or* half-and-half cream
1/2 teaspoon salt
1/4 teaspoon pepper
6 hard-cooked eggs, sliced
1 cup (4 ounces) shredded cheddar cheese
1 cup crushed potato chips

Place the asparagus in a large saucepan with enough water to cover; cook until crisp-tender. Drain well; set asparagus aside.

In a saucepan over medium heat, melt butter. Stir in flour until smooth. Gradually add milk. Bring to a boil over medium heat; cook and stir for 2 minutes. Add salt and pepper.

Layer half of the asparagus in an ungreased 11-in. x 7-in. x 2-in. baking dish. Cover with half of the eggs, cheese and sauce. Repeat layers. Sprinkle with potato chips. Bake, uncovered, at 350° for 30 minutes or until heated through. **Yield:** 6-8 servings.

Potato Rolls

*What better time to shape rolls into cloverleafs than for the celebration of St. Patrick's Day? I found this recipe in a magazine over 40 years ago. These rolls are well received at fellowship dinners and are also popular at home. They are the tastiest rolls I make.
      —Beatrice McGrath, Norridgewock, Maine*

1 package (1/4 ounce) active dry yeast
1/4 cup warm water (110° to 115°)
1 cup warm milk (110° to 115°)
1/4 cup shortening
1/2 cup warm mashed potatoes
1 egg
1/4 cup sugar
1-1/4 teaspoons salt
4 cups all-purpose flour

In a mixing bowl, dissolve yeast in water. Add milk, shortening, potatoes, egg, sugar, salt and 2 cups flour; beat until smooth. Add enough remaining flour to form a soft dough.

Turn onto a floured surface; knead until smooth and elastic, about 6-8 minutes. Place in a greased bowl, turning once to grease top. Cover and let rise in a warm place until doubled, about 1 hour.

Punch dough down and divide in half. Divide each half into 36 pieces; shape into balls. Place three balls each into greased muffin cups. Cover and let rise in a warm place until doubled, about 30 minutes. Bake at 400° for 12-15 minutes or until golden brown. Remove to wire racks. Serve warm. **Yield:** 2 dozen.

Spring Fruit Salad

I frequently choose this easy and elegant salad when planning a menu. The flavors blend nicely as it refrigerates. Also, it's nice to have the salad ready when you're busy with last-minute details of serving an entire meal.   —Karla Retzer, Grantsburg, Wisconsin

1 can (11 ounces) mandarin oranges, drained
1 cup flaked coconut, toasted
1 cup miniature marshmallows
1 can (8 ounces) pineapple tidbits, drained
1 cup (8 ounces) sour cream
2 tablespoons chopped walnuts
1 tablespoon brown sugar
Fresh mint, optional

In a bowl, combine the first five ingredients; mix well. Cover and refrigerate overnight. Just before serving, sprinkle with walnuts and brown sugar. Garnish with mint if desired. **Yield:** 6 servings.

Ham Hints

Choose firm, plump hams that are rosy pink and finely grained. Most hams are "fully cooked" and can be eaten immediately or heated until hot (140°). Some, however, are labeled "cook before eating" and must be cooked to an internal temperature of 160°.

Braised Beef Rolls

This is a great company dish because it can be fixed ahead. Everyone enjoys the old-fashioned sweet-sour flavor. —Mary Kay Ankney, Springfield, Oregon

      2 to 3 pounds London broil *or* flank steak rolls
  1/2 teaspoon salt
  1/4 teaspoon pepper
      2 tablespoons vegetable oil
  1-3/4 cups water, *divided*
  1/2 cup packed brown sugar
  1/2 cup raisins
      1 medium onion, cut into wedges
      2 tablespoons vinegar
      2 tablespoons lemon juice
      1 teaspoon ground mustard
      1 bay leaf, optional
      2 tablespoons all-purpose flour
Hot cooked rice

Sprinkle meat with salt and pepper. In a Dutch oven over medium heat, brown the meat on both sides in oil; drain.

Combine 1-1/2 cups of water, brown sugar, raisins, onion, vinegar, lemon juice, mustard and bay leaf if desired in a saucepan. Bring to a boil. Combine flour and remaining water until smooth; stir into raisin sauce. Bring to a boil; cook and stir for 2 minutes or until thickened. Pour over the meat rolls.

Cover and bake at 325° for 1-1/2 hours or until the meat is tender. Discard bay leaf. Serve over rice. **Yield:** 4-6 servings.

Cream of Mushroom Soup

My daughter-in-law, a gourmet cook, served this soup as the first course for a family dinner. She'd gotten the recipe from her mom and graciously shared it with me. —Anne Kulick, Phillipsburg, New Jersey

  1/4 cup chopped onion
      2 tablespoons butter *or* margarine
      3 cups sliced fresh mushrooms
      6 tablespoons all-purpose flour
      2 cans (14-1/2 ounces *each*) chicken broth
      1 cup half-and-half cream
  1/2 teaspoon salt
  1/8 teaspoon pepper

In a large saucepan, saute onion in butter until tender. Add mushrooms and saute until tender. Combine flour and broth until smooth; stir into the mushroom mixture.

Bring to a boil; cook and stir for 2 minutes or until thickened. Reduce heat. Stir in the cream, salt and pepper. Simmer, uncovered, for 15 minutes, stirring often. **Yield:** 4-6 servings.

Special Brussels Sprouts

I grew up on a farm in southern Louisiana, so we had fresh vegetables most of the year. Mother served brussels sprouts at least twice a week. Fresh from the garden, they were sweet and tender. Now I make this recipe all year using frozen sprouts. —Ruby Miguez Crowley, Louisiana

  1/4 cup sliced almonds
      1 tablespoon butter *or* margarine
      1 package (16 ounces) frozen brussels sprouts
      1 chicken bouillon cube
      1 can (10-3/4 ounces) condensed cream of chicken soup, undiluted
      2 tablespoons milk
      1 jar (2 ounces) chopped pimientos, drained
  1/4 teaspoon pepper
  1/8 teaspoon dried thyme

In a small skillet, saute almonds in butter until lightly browned; set aside. In a saucepan, cook brussels sprouts according to package directions, adding the bouillon cube to the water.

Meanwhile, in another saucepan, combine soup, milk, pimientos, pepper and thyme. Cook until heated through. Drain sprouts; top with cream sauce and stir gently. Sprinkle with almonds. **Yield:** 4-6 servings.

George Washington Cherry Cobbler

We lived on a farm with lots of fruit trees when I was growing up, and since Dad loved fruit, Mother prepared it often in many different ways. Blackberries or blueberries can also be used in this cobbler. —Juanita Sherwood, Charleston, Illinois

  1/2 cup sugar
      2 tablespoons cornstarch
  1/4 teaspoon ground cinnamon
  3/4 cup water
      1 package (12 ounces) frozen dark sweet cherries, thawed
      1 tablespoon butter *or* margarine
TOPPING:
      1 cup all-purpose flour
      4 tablespoons sugar, *divided*
      2 teaspoons baking powder
  1/2 teaspoon salt
      3 tablespoons shortening
  1/2 cup milk
Ice cream, optional

In a saucepan, combine sugar, cornstarch and cinnamon. Stir in water until smooth. Add the cherries and butter. Bring to a boil over medium heat, stirring frequently. Cook and stir for 2 minutes or until thickened. Pour into an 8-in. square baking pan; set aside.

In a bowl, combine flour, 2 tablespoons sugar, baking powder and salt. Cut in shortening until mixture resembles coarse crumbs. Stir in milk just until moistened. Drop by spoonfuls over the cherries; sprinkle with remaining sugar.

Bake at 400° for 30-35 minutes or until golden brown. Serve warm with ice cream if desired. **Yield:** 8 servings.

RECIPE FOR: *Cool Cucumber*

1 pkg (3oz) lime gelatin
½ tsp. salt
½ c. boiling

BUTTER ROAST CHICKEN
½ cup butter or m
Juice of 2 lemons
1 to 2 paprika
2 tsps. salt
1 tsp. pepper
1 tsp. brown
½ tsp. dried

Preparation time:

Recipe For: *Asparagus*
Serves: 6   Preparation
1½ pounds fresh asp
1½ inch piece
2 tablespoons butter
2 tablespoons all pu
½ teaspoon salt
¼ teaspoon pepper
1 cup milk

Butter Roast Chicken

When I was newly married, I was very interested in cooking, so I started to collect recipes. My new sister-in-law's mother sent me her family's favorite chicken recipe, and I knew it was destined to be a favorite in our household. —Elisabeth Garrison, Elmer, New Jersey

- 1 broiler-fryer chicken (2-1/2 to 3 pounds), cut up
- 1/2 cup butter *or* margarine
- 1/3 cup lemon juice
- 1 tablespoon paprika
- 2 teaspoons salt
- 1 teaspoon pepper
- 1 teaspoon brown sugar
- 1/2 teaspoon dried rosemary, crushed
- 1/8 teaspoon ground nutmeg
- 1/8 teaspoon cayenne pepper

Place chicken in an ungreased 13-in. x 9-in. x 2-in. baking pan. Combine remaining ingredients in a small saucepan; bring to a boil. Remove from the heat and pour over chicken. Bake, uncovered, at 325° for 1-1/2 hours or until juices run clear, basting occasionally. **Yield:** 6 servings.

Asparagus Supreme

We live in "The Garden State", and our produce is top-notch in season. Spring is the time to enjoy asparagus, and I prepare it several times a week. This is one of my favorite ways to use asparagus. —Elisabeth Garrison

- 1-1/2 pounds fresh asparagus, cut into 1-1/2-inch pieces
- 2 tablespoons butter *or* margarine
- 2 tablespoons all-purpose flour
- 1/2 teaspoon salt
- 1/4 teaspoon pepper
- 1 cup milk
- 4 hard-cooked eggs, diced
- 1 jar (2 ounces) diced pimientos, drained
- 1 cup (4 ounces) shredded cheddar cheese
Dry bread crumbs

Cook asparagus in boiling water until nearly tender; drain and set aside. In a small saucepan, melt butter. Add flour, salt and pepper; cook and stir until smooth and bubbly. Gradually add milk; cook and stir until thickened. Remove from the heat.

Place half of the asparagus in a greased 1-1/2-qt. baking dish. Top with half of the white sauce, eggs, pimientos and cheese. Repeat layers. Sprinkle with bread crumbs. Bake, uncovered, at 325° for 30-35 minutes. **Yield:** 6 servings.

Cool Cucumber Salad

This salad is a refreshing complement to any meal, and it's attractive on the table. Whenever I'm asked to bring a dish to a potluck dinner or family gathering, I prepare this salad. I often make it for friends and neighbors, too. It's always much appreciated.

—Elisabeth Garrison

- 1 medium cucumber
- 1 package (3 ounces) lime gelatin
- 1 teaspoon salt
- 1/2 cup boiling water
- 1 cup mayonnaise
- 1 cup cottage cheese
- 1 small onion, grated
Sliced cucumbers and fresh parsley, optional

Peel and halve cucumber; remove the seeds. Shred and pat dry; set aside.

In a bowl, combine gelatin and salt with boiling water; stir until dissolved. Add mayonnaise and cottage cheese; mix well. Stir in the onion and shredded cucumber.

Pour into a 5-cup mold coated with nonstick cooking spray. Refrigerate until firm. Unmold onto a serving platter. Garnish with cucumbers and parsley if desired. **Yield:** 6 servings.

Pineapple Cheesecake Squares

Everyone seems to love this dessert, perhaps because it's not too sweet-tasting. A cousin gave me the recipe a long time ago, much to the delight of my children, who always enjoyed it. It's both light and delicious.

—Elisabeth Garrison

- 1/2 cup all-purpose flour
- 3 tablespoons sugar
- 1/4 teaspoon salt
- 1/4 cup cold butter *or* margarine
FILLING:
- 1 can (8 ounces) crushed pineapple
- 1 package (8 ounces) cream cheese, softened
- 3 tablespoons sugar
- 1 tablespoon all-purpose flour
- 1 egg
- 1 cup milk
- 1 teaspoon vanilla extract
Ground cinnamon

In a bowl, combine the flour, sugar and salt; cut in the butter until crumbly. Press into the bottom of an ungreased 8-in. square baking pan. Bake at 325° for 12 minutes. Cool.

Meanwhile, drain pineapple, reserving juice; set pineapple and juice aside. In a mixing bowl, beat cream cheese, sugar and flour. Add egg and mix until smooth. Add pineapple juice. Gradually add milk and vanilla.

Sprinkle pineapple over crust. Slowly pour filling over pineapple. Sprinkle with cinnamon. Bake at 325° for 1 hour or until a knife inserted near the center comes out clean. Cool to room temperature. Chill; cut into squares. Refrigerate leftovers. **Yield:** 9 servings.

Corned Beef and Cabbage

Slices of this corned beef will put an Irish spring in everyone's step.   —*Evelyn Kenney, Trenton, New Jersey*

1 corned beef brisket (4 to 6 pounds)
2 tablespoons brown sugar
2 to 3 bay leaves
16 to 24 small potatoes, peeled
8 to 12 carrots, halved
1 large head cabbage, cut into wedges
HORSERADISH SAUCE:
3 tablespoons butter *or* margarine
2 tablespoons all-purpose flour
1 to 1-1/2 cups cooking liquid (from brisket)
1 tablespoon vinegar
1 tablespoon sugar
1/4 cup horseradish

Place brisket in a large Dutch oven; cover with water. Add brown sugar and bay leaves. (If a spice packet is enclosed with the brisket, add it also.) Bring to a boil. Reduce heat; cover and simmer for 2 hours.

Add potatoes and carrots. Return to boiling. Reduce heat; cover and simmer 30-40 minutes or until meat and vegetables are just tender. If Dutch oven is not large enough for cabbage to fit, remove potatoes and carrots and keep warm (they can be returned to cooking liquid and heated through before serving). Add cabbage; cover and cook 15 minutes or until tender.

Discard bay leaves. Remove cabbage and meat. If making Horseradish Sauce, strain and remove about 1-1/2 cups cooking liquid. Let meat stand a few minutes. Slice meat across the grain. Serve with Horseradish Sauce. **Yield:** 8-12 servings.

Horseradish Sauce: In a small saucepan, melt butter. Blend in flour. Add 1 cup cooking liquid; stir until smooth. Add vinegar, sugar and horseradish. Cook and stir over medium heat until thickened and bubbly. Adjust seasoning with additional vinegar, sugar or horseradish if needed. Thin sauce if necessary with the remaining cooking liquid. **Yield:** about 1-1/2 cups.

Irish Soda Bread

Some people consider bread to be the most important part of a meal ...and this bread just might satisfy such folks! It comes from an old recipe.   —*Evelyn Kenney*

4 cups all-purpose flour
1/4 cup sugar
1 teaspoon salt
1 teaspoon baking powder
1 teaspoon baking soda
1/4 cup butter *or* margarine
3 to 4 tablespoons caraway seed
2 cups raisins
1-1/3 cups buttermilk
1 egg, beaten
Milk

In a mixing bowl, combine flour, sugar, salt, baking powder and baking soda. Cut in butter until mixture resembles coarse crumbs. Stir in caraway seed and raisins. Combine buttermilk and egg; stir into dry ingredients just until moistened.

Turn onto a floured surface; knead lightly until smooth. Shape into a ball and place on a greased baking pan. Pat into a 7-in. round loaf. Cut a 4-in. cross about 1/4 in. deep on top. Brush top with milk. Bake at 375° for 1 hour or until golden brown. **Yield:** 1 loaf.

Beet Relish

I like to serve this relish with corned beef. It provides an interesting combination of flavors, and it is best made several days ahead.   —*Evelyn Kenney*

2 cups coarsely shredded cooked beets
2 tablespoons chopped red onion
2 tablespoons red wine vinegar *or* cider vinegar
1 teaspoon sugar
2 tablespoons Dijon mustard
3 tablespoons vegetable oil
Salt and pepper to taste

Combine all ingredients in a small bowl and blend well. Chill thoroughly. **Yield:** about 2 cups.

Emerald Isle Cake

This cake is so simple to make, and it provides the perfect finish for an Irish meal. The glaze adds just the right touch of sweetness, but even more importantly, it features the color of the day—green!   —*Evelyn Kenney*

1/2 cup butter *or* margarine, softened
1 cup sugar
2 eggs
1 teaspoon vanilla extract
1-3/4 cups all-purpose flour
2 teaspoons baking powder
1/2 teaspoon salt
1/2 cup milk
GLAZE:
1 cup confectioners' sugar
1 to 2 tablespoons milk *or* Irish whiskey
Green food coloring, optional
Slivered almonds, optional

In a mixing bowl, cream butter and sugar. Add eggs, one at a time, beating well after each addition. Blend in vanilla. Combine flour, baking powder and salt; add alternately with the milk. Beat until smooth. Spread into a greased 9-in. square baking pan. Bake at 350° for 40 minutes or until a toothpick inserted near the center comes out clean.

For glaze, combine confectioners' sugar and milk or whiskey; stir until smooth and fairly thin. If desired, add 1 to 2 drops of food coloring and stir until well blended. Spread glaze over warm cake. Sprinkle with almonds if desired. **Yield:** 9-12 servings.

Ham Cups with Cherry Sauce

This recipe is my family's traditional Easter entree. The individual cups are pretty on the plate, especially when topped with the bright cherry sauce. Since we raise pigs, we have a good pork supply.
—Ellen Martin, Oxford, New Jersey

1 egg
1-1/2 cups soft bread crumbs
1/2 teaspoon ground mustard
1 pound ground fully cooked ham
1/2 pound ground pork
1/4 cup packed brown sugar
1 teaspoon prepared mustard
CHERRY SAUCE:
2 tablespoons cornstarch
1/2 cup sugar
1 can (16 ounces) pitted red cherries, undrained
Red food coloring, optional

In a bowl, combine egg, bread crumbs and ground mustard. Add ham and pork; mix well. Shape into eight equal portions; pat lightly into 2-3/4-in. muffin cups. Combine brown sugar and prepared mustard; sprinkle over cups. Bake at 350° for 40 minutes or until no longer pink.

For sauce, combine cornstarch and sugar in a saucepan. Add cherries; cook and stir over medium-high heat until thickened and bubbly. Cook and stir 2 minutes longer. If desired, stir in 4-5 drops food coloring. Serve over ham cups. **Yield:** 6 servings.

Macaroni Au Gratin

Here's an easy, tasty dish my family has always liked. Whenever we attend a potluck supper, I take this macaroni casserole...and come home with an empty dish and many requests for the recipe. —Jeannine Hopp
Menomonee Falls, Wisconsin

1 package (7 ounces) macaroni
1/4 cup butter *or* margarine
1/4 cup all-purpose flour
2 cups milk
8 ounces process American cheese, cubed
1 tablespoon chopped onion
1/2 teaspoon Worcestershire sauce
1/2 teaspoon salt
1/4 teaspoon pepper
1/4 teaspoon ground mustard
2 tablespoons Italian-seasoned bread crumbs

Cook macaroni according to package directions; drain. Place in a greased 2-qt. baking dish; set aside.

In a saucepan, melt butter over medium heat. Stir in flour until well blended. Gradually add milk; bring to a boil. Cook and stir for 2 minutes; reduce heat. Add cheese, onion, Worcestershire sauce, salt, pepper and mustard; stir until cheese melts.

Pour over macaroni and mix well. Sprinkle with bread crumbs. Bake, uncovered, at 375° for 30 minutes. **Yield:** 6 servings.

Orange Buttermilk Salad

My family absolutely loves this gelatin salad, and I do, too, because it's so easy to make! The buttermilk adds a wonderful tang, making it a refreshing accompaniment to most any meal.
—Lenore Wilson
Muskogee, Oklahoma

1 can (20 ounces) crushed pineapple
1 package (6 ounces) orange gelatin
2 cups buttermilk
1 carton (8 ounces) frozen whipped topping, thawed

In a saucepan, bring pineapple with juice to a boil. Stir in the gelatin until dissolved. Remove from the heat; stir in buttermilk. Cool to room temperature.

Fold in whipped topping. Pour into an 11-in. x 7-in. x 2-in. dish or 2-qt. bowl. Chill for at least 4 hours. **Yield:** 10 servings.

Rhubarb Peach Shortcake

I received this recipe years ago from my mother. It's one of the first desserts I make in the spring when our fresh rhubarb comes in. I discovered rhubarb and peaches go well together, and the biscuits make it a hearty dessert. —Sheila Butler, Kansas City, Missouri

1/4 cup packed brown sugar
1 tablespoon cornstarch
1 can (16 ounces) sliced peaches
2 cups chopped fresh *or* frozen rhubarb
1/2 teaspoon vanilla extract
1 tube (5 to 6 ounces) refrigerated buttermilk biscuits
1 tablespoon sugar

In a saucepan, combine brown sugar and cornstarch. Drain peaches, reserving 1/2 cup liquid. Set peaches aside. Stir reserved liquid into brown sugar mixture; bring to a boil. Cook and stir for 2 minutes. Add rhubarb; simmer for 8 minutes. Stir in peaches and vanilla. Pour into an ungreased 8-in. round baking pan.

Dip one side of biscuits in sugar; place over hot fruit with sugar side up. Bake, uncovered, at 375° for 20-24 minutes or until biscuits are golden brown. Serve warm. **Yield:** 5 servings.

Rhubarb Tips

Rhubarb should have crisp, brightly hued stalks. The leaves should be fresh looking and blemish free. Rhubarb lovers can enjoy it out of season by cutting it into 1-inch chunks and freezing in a freezer-proof plastic bag for up to 9 months.

Broiled Fish

This fish is the first meal my mom made for me when I came home after I graduated from college. Her secret in preparing this recipe was to butter the fish first before dusting it with flour. That seals in the moisture of the fish, which makes it succulent and absolutely delicious.
—Ann Berg, Chesapeake, Virginia

    4 orange roughy, red snapper, catfish *or* trout
      fillets (1-1/2 to 2 pounds)
    6 tablespoons butter *or* margarine, melted,
      divided
    1 tablespoon all-purpose flour
Paprika
Juice of 1 lemon
    1 tablespoon minced fresh parsley
    2 teaspoons Worcestershire sauce

Place fish on a broiler rack that has been coated with nonstick cooking spray. Brush tops of fish with 3 table-spoons of the butter; dust with flour and sprinkle with paprika. Broil 5-6 in. from the heat for 5 minutes or until fish just begins to brown.

Combine lemon juice, parsley, Worcestershire sauce and remaining butter; pour over the fish. Broil 5 minutes longer or until fish flakes easily with a fork. **Yield:** 4 servings.

Roasted New Potatoes

This simple recipe is anything but plain. The flavors of garlic and herbs combine to add extra zip to tender new potatoes. This side dish goes hand in hand with the delicate taste of fish.
—Ann Berg

1-1/2 pounds new potatoes, quartered
    2 tablespoons olive *or* vegetable oil
    2 garlic cloves, minced
    1/2 teaspoon dried rosemary, crushed
    1/2 teaspoon dried thyme
    1/2 teaspoon salt
    1/8 teaspoon pepper

Combine all of the ingredients in a large plastic bag; toss to coat. Pour into an ungreased 13-in. x 9-in. x 2-in. baking pan. Bake, uncovered, at 450° for 35 minutes or until potatoes are tender. Remove from the oven and cover with foil to keep warm while broiling fish. **Yield:** 4 servings.

Blue Cheese Salad

A fresh salad is the perfect complement to any meal, but this colorful combination has eye appeal as well. I love the crispy crunch of croutons and tangy touch of dill in this recipe.
—Ann Berg

    1/4 cup white wine vinegar *or* cider
      vinegar
    1/4 cup olive *or* vegetable oil
    1 garlic clove, minced

    1/4 teaspoon pepper
    1/4 teaspoon seasoned salt
    1/2 teaspoon dill weed
    1 small bunch romaine, torn
    3 hard-cooked eggs, chopped
    1 cup croutons
    1/2 cup crumbled blue cheese

In a small bowl or jar with a tight-fitting lid, combine the first six ingredients; mix or shake until dressing is well blended.

Place the romaine in a large salad bowl; top with the eggs, croutons and blue cheese. Add the salad dressing and toss to coat. Serve immediately. **Yield:** 4 servings.

Baked Lemon Pudding

The tart taste of lemon brings the perfect finish to this meal. It was always a treat when Mother made this scrumptious dessert. It's light, luscious and lovely.
—Ann Berg

    1 cup sugar
    3 tablespoons all-purpose flour
    3/4 cup milk
Juice of 2 lemons, strained
    1 tablespoon butter *or* margarine, melted
    2 teaspoons grated lemon peel
    2 eggs, *separated*

In a medium bowl, combine sugar and flour. Stir in milk, lemon juice, butter and lemon peel. Beat egg yolks; add to the lemon mixture. Beat egg whites until stiff peaks form; fold into the lemon mixture.

Pour into a greased 1-qt. baking dish; set in a larger pan with 1/2 in. of water. Bake, uncovered, at 350° for 55-60 minutes. Serve warm. Refrigerate any leftovers. **Yield:** 4 servings.

Fish Facts

Fish fillets and steaks should have a fresh odor, firm texture and moist appearance. Immediately refrigerate fresh fish, tightly wrapped, and use within a day or two.

To test fish for doneness, gently prod it with a fork at its thickest point. Properly cooked fish is opaque, has milky white juices and flakes easily. Under-cooked fish is still translucent and the juices are clear and watery.

Leftover fish makes a delicious salad the next day. Cut the fish into chunks and marinate it overnight in salad dressing; drain and serve over greens.

Tasty Sloppy Joes

These sandwiches have been a hit with my family from the first time I served them years ago. They make a quick hearty meal along with soup or a salad. I like to make a large batch and freeze the leftovers.
—*Pauline Schrock, Sullivan, Illinois*

1-1/2 pounds lean ground beef
   1 cup milk
   3/4 cup quick-cooking oats
   1 medium onion, chopped
   1 tablespoon Worcestershire sauce
1-1/2 teaspoons salt
   1/4 teaspoon pepper
   1 cup ketchup
   1/2 cup water
   3 tablespoons white vinegar
   2 tablespoons sugar
  10 sandwich buns, split

In a large skillet over medium heat, cook the beef, milk, oats, onion, Worcestershire sauce, salt and pepper until meat is no longer pink. Transfer to an ungreased 8-in. square baking dish.

Combine the ketchup, water, vinegar and sugar; pour over meat mixture. Bake, uncovered, at 350° for 45 minutes, stirring every 15 minutes. Spoon about 1/2 cup into each bun. **Yield:** 10 servings.

Cheddar Mushroom Macaroni

This is my favorite dish to bring to church dinners, and whenever we have a carry-in at work, I'm asked to make it. I discovered the recipe several years ago. The rich creamy taste keeps it on my list of favorites.
—*Barbara Williams, Shady Dale, Georgia*

4 cups (16 ounces) shredded cheddar cheese
1 can (10-3/4 ounces) condensed cream of
   mushroom soup, undiluted
1 cup mayonnaise*
1 can (7 ounces) mushroom stems and pieces,
   drained
1 medium onion, finely chopped
1 jar (2 ounces) diced pimientos, drained
4 cups cooked elbow macaroni
1 garlic clove, minced, optional

In a large bowl, combine the first six ingredients; mix well. Stir in macaroni and garlic if desired. Transfer to a greased 2-1/2-qt. baking dish. Cover and bake at 325° for 30 minutes or until heated through and cheese is melted. **Yield:** 6-8 servings.

*Editor's Note: Reduced-fat or fat-free mayonnaise is not recommended for this recipe.

Basil Dill Coleslaw

I was first introduced to basil when I married into an Italian family. I loved the aromatic fragrance and fla-
vor of the fresh herb and began to use it in just about everything. Basil and dill add a unique touch to this refreshing cabbage slaw. It's great served alongside a variety of entrees.
—*June Cappetto*
Seattle, Washington

6 cups shredded cabbage
3 to 4 tablespoons chopped fresh basil *or* 1
   tablespoon dried basil
3 tablespoons snipped fresh dill *or* 1
   tablespoon dill weed
DRESSING:
  1/2 cup mayonnaise
   3 tablespoons sugar
   2 tablespoons cider vinegar
   2 tablespoons half-and-half cream
   1 teaspoon coarsely ground pepper

In a serving bowl, combine the cabbage, basil and dill. In a small bowl, combine all of the dressing ingredients until blended. Pour over the cabbage mixture and toss to coat. Cover and refrigerate until serving. **Yield:** 6-8 servings.

White Chocolate Chip Hazelnut Cookies

This is a cookie you will want to make again and again. I like to take it to church get-togethers and family reunions. It's very delicious...crispy on the outside and chewy on the inside. I'm always asked to share a copy of the recipe.
—*Denise DeJong*
Pittsburgh, Pennsylvania

1-1/4 cups whole hazelnuts, toasted, *divided*
   9 tablespoons butter *or* margarine, softened,
     divided
  1/2 cup sugar
  1/2 cup packed brown sugar
   1 egg
   1 teaspoon vanilla extract
1-1/2 cups all-purpose flour
  1/2 teaspoon baking soda
  1/2 teaspoon salt
   1 cup white *or* vanilla chips

Coarsely chop 1/2 cup hazelnuts and set aside. Melt 2 tablespoons butter. In a food processor, combine the melted butter and the remaining hazelnuts. Cover and process until the mixture forms a crumbly paste; set aside.

In a mixing bowl, cream the remaining butter. Beat in the sugar and brown sugar. Add the egg and vanilla extract; beat until light and fluffy. Beat in the ground hazelnut mixture until blended. Combine the flour, baking soda and salt; add to the batter and mix just until combined. Stir in the white or vanilla chips and chopped hazelnuts.

Drop the dough by rounded tablespoonfuls 2 in. apart onto greased baking sheets. Bake at 350° for 10-12 minutes or until the cookies are lightly browned. Remove cookies to wire racks to cool completely. **Yield:** 3 dozen.

Pork Roast with Spiced Apples

The fine flavor of this pork roast is further enhanced when spicy-sweet apples are spooned over slices of the meat. This wonderful recipe made pork my favorite of all meats.   *—Oma Rollison, El Cajon, California*

  1 teaspoon salt
  1 teaspoon ground ginger
1/2 teaspoon ground nutmeg
1/2 teaspoon ground cinnamon
  1 boneless rolled pork loin roast (4 to 5
    pounds)
SPICED APPLES:
1/4 cup honey
1/2 cup water
  1 tablespoon lemon juice
1/4 teaspoon ground ginger
1/4 teaspoon ground nutmeg
1/4 teaspoon ground cinnamon
  2 medium apples, peeled, cored and sliced

Combine salt, ginger, nutmeg and cinnamon; rub over roast. Place roast, fat side up, on a rack in a shallow roasting pan. Bake, uncovered, at 325° for 2 to 2-1/2 hours or until a meat thermometer reads 160°. Cover and let stand 15 minutes before slicing.

In a medium skillet, combine the first six spiced apples ingredients; bring to a boil. Reduce heat and simmer, uncovered, until slightly thickened. Add apples; simmer, uncovered, until apples are just tender, stirring gently. Serve with sliced pork roast. **Yield:** 8-10 servings.

Sweet-and-Sour Green Beans

These beans are the perfect accompaniment to the pork roast. The flavors are compatible and blend well. I've never cooked any other vegetable dish when I make this pork roast dinner.   *—Oma Rollison*

  4 bacon strips
1/2 cup chopped onion
  2 tablespoons all-purpose flour
3/4 cup water
1/3 cup cider vinegar
  2 tablespoons sugar
  6 to 8 cups green beans, cooked and drained

In a skillet, cook bacon until crisp; drain, reserving 2 tablespoons of drippings. Crumble the bacon and set aside. Saute the onion in drippings until tender.

Stir in flour until thoroughly combined. Add water, vinegar and sugar. Cook and stir until thickened and bubbly; cook and stir 2 minutes more. Gently stir in beans and heat through. Sprinkle with bacon. Serve immediately. **Yield:** 8-10 servings.

Spoon Rolls

Since the batter may be stored in the refrigerator for up to 4 days, this is a wonderful way to treat your family

to homemade rolls without the extra preparation each time. My mother raised eight children, and we had these delicious from-scratch rolls often.   *—Oma Rollison*

  1 package (1/4 ounce) active dry yeast
  2 cups warm water (110° to 115°)
1/2 cup butter *or* margarine, melted
  1 egg, beaten
1/4 cup sugar
  4 cups self-rising flour*

In a large mixing bowl, dissolve yeast in warm water. Let stand for 5 minutes. Add butter, egg and sugar; mix well. Stir in flour until thoroughly combined (batter will be soft). Cover and refrigerate overnight. Spoon batter into greased or paper-lined muffin cups. Bake at 375° for 25-30 minutes or until golden brown. **Yield:** 16 rolls.

*Editor's Note: As a substitute for each cup of self-rising flour, place 1-1/2 teaspoons baking powder and 1/2 teaspoon salt in a measuring cup. Add all-purpose flour to measure 1 cup.

Bananas 'n' Cream Bundt Cake

This absolutely scrumptious cake needs no icing…just a dusting of powdered sugar.   *—Oma Rollison*

   1/3 cup shortening
1-1/4 cups sugar
    2 eggs
    1 teaspoon vanilla extract
1-1/4 cups mashed ripe bananas (about 3 medium)
    2 cups all-purpose flour
1-1/4 teaspoons baking powder
    1 teaspoon baking soda
   1/2 teaspoon salt
    1 cup (8 ounces) sour cream
   3/4 cup chopped walnuts
Confectioners' sugar

In a mixing bowl, cream the shortening and sugar. Add the eggs, one at a time, beating well after each addition. Blend in vanilla. Add bananas and mix well. Combine flour, baking powder, baking soda and salt; add to the creamed mixture alternately with sour cream, stirring just until combined. Stir in walnuts.

Pour into a greased and floured 10-in. fluted tube pan. Bake at 350° for 50 minutes or until a toothpick comes out clean. Cool 10 minutes in pan before removing to a wire rack to cool completely. Dust with confectioners' sugar. **Yield:** 12-16 servings.

Banana Basics

Store ripe bananas in a sealed plastic bag in the refrigerator. The peel will turn brown but the flesh will remain unchanged.

Ham 'n' Egg Casserole

I like to prepare this when I have leftovers of ham and day-old bread on hand. It's a delicious dish for brunch. Besides being so tasty, it's prepared the night before, which allows me more time to complete other dishes for the meal. —Elizabeth Hesse, Springville, New York

    1/2 cup chopped green pepper
    1/2 cup butter *or* margarine
     10 slices white bread, cubed
      2 cups cubed fully cooked ham
    1/2 pound process American cheese, cubed
      6 eggs
      2 cups milk
      1 teaspoon ground mustard

In a skillet, saute green pepper in butter until tender. Remove green pepper, reserving drippings. Combine green pepper, bread and ham; place in an ungreased 13-in. x 9-in. x 2-in. baking dish.

Add cheese to drippings; cook and stir over low heat until cheese melts. Pour over bread mixture. Beat eggs, milk and mustard; pour over cheese. Cover and refrigerate overnight. Remove from the refrigerator 30 minutes before baking. Bake, uncovered, at 300° for 1 hour. **Yield:** 10-12 servings.

Blue-Ribbon Doughnuts

I received this recipe from my sister about 30 years ago. Our eight children are grown and no longer live at home, but I'm still making these doughnuts—they've become a favorite with my grandchildren! They can't seem to get enough of these tasty treats.
—Kay McEwen, Sussex, New Brunswick

      3 eggs
      2 cups sugar
      1 cup heavy whipping cream
      1 cup milk
      1 teaspoon vanilla extract
    6 to 7 cups all-purpose flour
      4 teaspoons cream of tartar
      2 teaspoons baking soda
      1 teaspoon salt
      1 teaspoon ground nutmeg
    Oil for deep-fat frying

In a mixing bowl, beat eggs for 5 minutes. Gradually beat in sugar; beat 1-2 minutes longer (mixture will be thick and light in color). Add cream, milk, vanilla, 2 cups flour, cream of tartar, baking soda, salt and nutmeg; beat until smooth. Add enough remaining flour to form a soft dough.

Turn onto a floured surface; knead until smooth, about 8-10 minutes. Place in a greased bowl, turning once to grease top. Cover and chill for 2-3 hours.

Roll on a floured surface to 1/2-in. thickness. Cut with a 2-1/2-in. doughnut cutter. In an electric skillet or deep-fat fryer, heat oil to 375°. Fry doughnuts, a few at a time, for 2 minutes per side or until browned. Drain on paper towels. **Yield:** 3 dozen.

Old-World Puff Pancake

My mom told me her mother-in-law showed her how to make this dish, which became popular during the Depression, on their "get acquainted" visit in 1927. At that time, cooks measured ingredients as pinches, dashes and dibs. But through the years, accurate amounts were noted. My wife and I continue to enjoy this dish today, particularly for brunch. —Auton Miller
Piney Flats, Tennessee

      2 tablespoons butter *or* margarine
      3 eggs
    3/4 cup milk
    3/4 cup all-purpose flour
      2 teaspoons sugar
      1 teaspoon ground nutmeg
    Confectioners' sugar
    Lemon wedges
    Maple syrup, optional

Place butter in a 10-in. ovenproof skillet; place in a 425° oven for 2-3 minutes or until melted. In a blender, process the eggs, milk, flour, sugar and nutmeg until smooth. Pour into prepared skillet.

Bake at 425° for 16-18 minutes or until puffed and browned. Dust with confectioners' sugar. Serve with lemon wedges and maple syrup if desired. **Yield:** 4-6 servings.

Creamy Fruit Bowl

This creamy fruit salad is always on the menu for special occasions, since it can be served as either a salad or dessert. When one of us brings it to a gathering, we take a copy of the recipe along to share, since someone always requests it! —Gretchen Baudhuin
Palm Coast, Florida

      1 can (20 ounces) pineapple tidbits
      3 egg yolks, beaten
      2 tablespoons sugar
      2 tablespoons vinegar
      1 tablespoon butter *or* margarine
    Dash salt
      4 oranges, sectioned, *divided*
      3 cups seedless grapes, *divided*
      2 cups miniature marshmallows
      1 cup heavy whipping cream, whipped
    Fresh mint, optional

Drain the pineapple, reserving 2 tablespoons juice; set pineapple aside. Pour the juice into the top of a double boiler; add the egg yolks, sugar, vinegar, butter and salt. Cook and stir over medium-low heat until the mixture thickens and coats the back of a spoon. Cool.

Stir in the pineapple, three oranges, 2-1/2 cups grapes and marshmallows. Cover and chill for at least 12 hours.

Fold in whipped cream just before serving. Top with remaining oranges and grapes. Garnish with mint if desired. **Yield:** 10-12 servings.

Leg of Lamb

My mother's baked leg of lamb was a masterpiece! Our family always looked forward to having it on Easter Sunday. —Barbara Tierney, Farmington, Connecticut

 1/2 leg of lamb (3 to 4 pounds)
  5 garlic cloves, minced
  1 teaspoon *each* salt and pepper
 1/4 teaspoon ground thyme
 1/4 teaspoon garlic powder
 1/4 cup all-purpose flour

Cut five slits in the meat; insert garlic. Combine salt, pepper, thyme and garlic powder; rub over meat. Place on a rack in a roasting pan. Broil 5-6 in. from the heat until browned; turn and brown the other side. Turn oven to 350°. Add 1/2 cup water to pan. Cover and bake for 25 minutes per pound or until internal temperature reaches 160° for medium or 170° for well-done.

Remove to carving board; keep warm. Pour pan drippings into a large measuring cup, scraping browned bits. Skim fat, reserving 1/4 cup in a saucepan; add flour. Add water to drippings to equal 2 cups; add all at once to flour mixture. Bring to a boil; cook and stir until thickened and bubbly. Cook and stir 1-2 minutes more. Slice lamb; serve with gravy. **Yield:** 6-8 servings.

Mixed Greens Salad

This was our family's favorite salad. A perfect complement to our Easter meal, it's light, crisp and refreshing. —Barbara Tierney

 1/2 small head iceberg lettuce, torn
 1/2 small bunch escarole *or* endive, torn
 1/2 small bunch Romaine, torn
  1 small tomato, cut into chunks
 1/2 small cucumber, sliced
 1/4 cup olive *or* vegetable oil
 1/4 cup red wine vinegar *or* cider vinegar
 1/4 teaspoon *each* salt and pepper

In a large salad bowl, toss greens, tomato and cucumber. Combine remaining ingredients in a jar with a tight-fitting lid; shake well. Pour over salad and toss. Serve immediately. **Yield:** 6-8 servings.

Mother's Manicotti

Manicotti was served as a first course. Instead of using pasta, Mother made crepes. —Barbara Tierney

CREPES:
  1 cup all-purpose flour
  1 cup water
  2 eggs
  1 tablespoon vegetable oil
Dash salt
FILLING:
  1 carton (15 ounces) ricotta cheese
 3/4 cup shredded mozzarella cheese
  3 tablespoons grated Parmesan cheese
  1 tablespoon chopped fresh parsley
  1 egg, beaten
  1 jar (28 ounces) spaghetti sauce
Additional shredded Parmesan cheese

Place flour in a bowl; whisk in water, eggs, oil and salt until smooth. Pour a generous 1/8 cup into a greased hot 8-in. skillet; turn to coat. Cook over medium heat until set; do not brown. Repeat with remaining batter. Stack crepes between waxed paper; set aside.

For filling, combine the cheeses, parsley and egg; mix well. Spread half the spaghetti sauce in the bottom of a 12-in. x 8-in. x 2-in. baking dish. Spoon 3 tablespoons of the cheese mixture down the center of each crepe; roll up. Place seam side down over spaghetti sauce; pour remaining sauce over crepes. Sprinkle with Parmesan cheese. Bake, uncovered, at 350° for 30 minutes or until bubbly. **Yield:** 6-8 servings.

Easter Pie

Easter pie is a specialty in many Italian homes, so mothers make sure their daughters master the recipe to ensure that the tradition continues. —Barbara Tierney

CRUST:
1-2/3 cups all-purpose flour
  2 tablespoons sugar
 1/2 teaspoon salt
 1/4 teaspoon baking powder
 1/4 cup cold butter *or* margarine
 1/4 cup shortening
  2 eggs, lightly beaten
FILLING:
  1 carton (15 ounces) ricotta cheese
  1 cup sugar
  1 tablespoon all-purpose flour
 1/4 teaspoon grated lemon peel
 1/4 teaspoon grated orange peel
Dash salt
  4 eggs
  2 teaspoons vanilla extract
 1/3 cup semisweet chocolate chips
 1/3 cup diced citron, optional
 1/8 teaspoon ground cinnamon
Dash ground nutmeg

In a bowl, combine the flour, sugar, salt and baking powder; cut in butter and shortening until mixture resembles small crumbs. Add eggs; stir until moistened and mixture forms a ball. Cover and refrigerate for 1 hour. On a lightly floured surface, roll out dough to a 10-in. circle. Place in a 9-in. pie plate; flute crust. Refrigerate.

For filling, beat the ricotta, sugar and flour in a mixing bowl. Add peels and salt; beat until smooth. In another bowl, beat eggs until thick and lemon-colored, about 5 minutes; slowly fold into ricotta mixture. Gently mix in remaining ingredients. Pour into the crust.

Bake at 350° for 55 minutes or until a knife inserted near the center comes out clean. Cool. Store in the refrigerator. **Yield:** 6-8 servings.

Deep-Dish Chicken Potpie

I adapted this recipe from a cookbook that I have had for many years. It's an excellent way to use up leftover chicken. Sometimes I make small individual pies and freeze them to have on hand.   —Bonnie Jean Lintick Kathyrn, Alberta

2 cups all-purpose flour
1/4 teaspoon salt
2/3 cup cold butter *or* margarine
1/4 cup cold water
FILLING:
2-1/2 cups cubed cooked chicken
2 cups fresh *or* frozen peas
2 medium potatoes, peeled and cubed
3 medium carrots, thinly sliced
2 celery ribs, finely chopped
1/4 cup finely chopped onion
3 tablespoons butter *or* margarine
3 tablespoons all-purpose flour
1 to 2 tablespoons chicken bouillon granules
1-1/2 teaspoons dried tarragon
Pepper to taste
1 cup milk
1/2 cup chicken broth
Additional milk

In a bowl, combine flour and salt; cut in butter until crumbly. Gradually add water, tossing with a fork until dough forms a ball. Set aside a third of the dough. Roll out remaining dough to fit a 2-1/2-qt. baking dish. Transfer pastry to baking dish. Trim even with edge; set aside.

For filling, in a bowl, combine the chicken, peas, potatoes, carrots, celery and onion; set aside. In a saucepan, melt butter. Stir in flour, bouillon, tarragon and pepper until smooth. Gradually stir in the milk and broth. Bring to a boil; cook and stir for 2 minutes or until thickened. Stir into chicken mixture; spoon into crust.

Roll out reserved dough to fit top of pie. Make cutouts in pastry. Place over filling; trim, seal and flute edges. Brush additional milk over pastry. Bake at 375° for 50-60 minutes or until crust is golden brown and filling is bubbly. **Yield:** 6 servings.

Ginger Pear Gelatin

This salad is among my favorites for special dinners. I love to cook and experiment with recipes, and I came up with this one after trying different combinations of fruits. The tangy taste is nice and refreshing.
*   —Sunnye Tiedemann, Bartlesville, Oklahoma*

1 package (3 ounces) lemon gelatin
1 cup boiling water
1 cup chilled ginger ale
1 can (15-1/4 ounces) pear halves, drained and cubed
1 cup halved green grapes

In a bowl, dissolve gelatin in boiling water. Stir in ginger ale. Cover and refrigerate until partially set. Stir in pears and grapes. Pour into a serving bowl. Chill until set. **Yield:** 6 servings.

Fruit Cooler

I especially enjoy this great pick-me-up drink after I have spent hours working out in the yard. By adding ice cubes while blending, I make a slushy version, which is refreshing when friends stop by or I'm just sitting on the porch relaxing.   —Frann Clark, DeRidder, Louisiana

2 cups orange juice
1 cup pineapple juice
1-1/2 cups fresh strawberries
1/4 cup confectioners' sugar
1 cup chilled carbonated water

In a blender, combine the orange and pineapple juices, strawberries and sugar. Cover and process until smooth. Transfer to a pitcher; stir in water. Serve on ice. **Yield:** 6 servings.

Orange Chiffon Cake

This cake recipe was given to me by my sister-in-law many years ago. It's deliciously light in texture, compatible with any meal and makes a beautiful presentation for special occasions.
*   —Ann Pitt Mountainside, New Jersey*

2 cups all-purpose flour
1-1/2 cups sugar
3 teaspoons baking powder
1/4 teaspoon salt
7 eggs, *separated*
1/2 cup orange juice
1/2 cup vegetable oil
1/4 cup water
2 teaspoons vanilla extract
1 tablespoon grated orange peel
2 teaspoons grated lemon peel
1/2 teaspoon cream of tartar
ICING:
1/2 cup confectioners' sugar
2 tablespoons shortening
1 tablespoon butter *or* margarine, softened
1 can (8 ounces) crushed pineapple, well drained

Sift the flour, sugar, baking powder and salt into a large bowl; make a well in the center. In another bowl, beat egg yolks until thick and lemon-colored. Beat in the orange juice, oil, water, vanilla, and orange and lemon peels. Pour into well in dry ingredients; beat with a wooden spoon until smooth. In a mixing bowl, beat egg whites on medium speed until foamy. Add cream of tartar; beat until stiff peaks form. Gradually fold into batter.

Transfer to an ungreased 10-in. tube pan. Bake at 325° for 55-60 minutes or until cake springs back when lightly touched. Immediately invert cake; cool completely. Loosen cake from sides of pan; remove cake and place on a serving platter.

For icing, combine the confectioners' sugar, shortening and butter until smooth. Spread over top of cake. Spoon pineapple over icing. **Yield:** 12 servings.

Steak Over Potatoes

I enjoy preparing this dish since it is one of the easiest, hearty meals I serve…so tasty, too. The chicken gumbo soup adds a unique flavor to the rest of the ingredients.
—Dennis Robinson, Laurel, Montana

2-1/2 pounds beef round steak
   1 can (10-3/4 ounces) condensed cream of
     onion soup, undiluted
   1 can (10-1/2 ounces) condensed chicken
     gumbo soup, undiluted
  1/4 teaspoon pepper
   8 baking potatoes

Cut steak into 3-in. x 1/4-in. strips; place in a bowl. Stir in soups and pepper. Transfer to a greased 2-1/2-qt. baking dish. Cover and bake at 350° for 30 minutes.

Add potatoes to the oven. Bake for 1-1/2 hours or until meat and potatoes are tender. Serve steak over potatoes. **Yield:** 8 servings.

Buttery Carrots 'n' Onions

My mother served this attractive side dish for all her special dinners, so I've been eating carrots this way since I was a child. Even my dinner guests who aren't too fond of carrots ask for this recipe. The added sweetness from the honey is a pleasant surprise. *—Joanie Elbourn*
Gardner, Massachusetts

   1 pound carrots, cut into 1/4-inch slices
1-1/4 cups water, *divided*
   1 teaspoon chicken bouillon granules
   3 medium onions, sliced and separated into
     rings
   2 tablespoons butter *or* margarine
   1 tablespoon all-purpose flour
   1 teaspoon salt
   1 teaspoon honey
  1/4 teaspoon sugar
Dash pepper

In a saucepan, combine carrots, 1/2 cup water and bouillon. Bring to a boil. Reduce heat; cover and cook for 5 minutes or until carrots are crisp-tender. Drain, reserving cooking liquid. Set carrots aside and keep warm.

In a large skillet, saute onions in butter for 10 minutes. Sprinkle with flour; stir until blended. Stir in the salt, honey, sugar, pepper and reserved cooking liquid until blended. Add remaining water; bring to a boil. Reduce heat; simmer, uncovered, for 10 minutes. Stir in carrots; heat through. **Yield:** 8-10 servings.

Salad with Tomato–Green Pepper Dressing

The longer this dressing is refrigerated, the more flavorful it becomes. The bright red-orange color is a sharp contrast to salad greens. At my house, it's everybody's favorite salad topping. *—Virginia Broten*
Pinewood, Minnesota

   1 can (10-3/4 ounces) condensed tomato
     soup, undiluted
  3/4 cup sugar
  2/3 cup cider vinegar
  1/2 cup vegetable oil
   1 large green pepper, cut into chunks
  1/2 medium onion, cut into chunks
   1 garlic clove, halved
   1 teaspoon ground mustard
  1/2 teaspoon salt
  1/2 teaspoon paprika
Salad greens and vegetables of your choice

In a blender, combine the first 10 ingredients; cover and process until smooth. Serve over tossed salad. Store leftovers in the refrigerator; shake before using. **Yield:** 4 cups dressing.

Crisp Lemon Sugar Cookies

I have had this recipe for about 40 years, and in that time I've made a few changes. These cookies are my husband's favorite, so I bake them for him almost every week. *—Dollie Ainley, Doniphan, Missouri*

  1/2 cup butter *or* margarine, softened
  1/2 cup butter-flavored shortening
   1 cup sugar
   1 egg
   1 tablespoon milk
   2 teaspoons lemon extract
   1 teaspoon vanilla extract
2-1/2 cups all-purpose flour
  3/4 teaspoon salt
  1/2 teaspoon baking soda
Additional sugar

In a mixing bowl, cream butter, shortening and sugar. Beat in egg, milk and extracts. Combine the flour, salt and baking soda; gradually add to creamed mixture.

Shape into 1-in. balls or drop by rounded teaspoonfuls 2 in. apart onto ungreased baking sheets. Flatten with a glass dipped in sugar. Bake at 400° for 9-11 minutes or until edges are lightly browned. Immediately remove to wire racks to cool. **Yield:** about 6-1/2 dozen.

Hot Potato Pointers

Russet potatoes are best for baking. Scrub well, blot dry with paper towels and use the tines of a fork to pierce potatoes about 1 inch deep in several places to let the steam out during baking.

If you rub a little butter or oil on the skin, it will be crisper and browner. Oiled potatoes also bake slightly faster. Place potatoes right on the oven rack.

pp. 34-35

pp. 42-43

pp. 44-45

pp. 50-51

Summer Meals

Baked Lemon Chicken • Green Beans with Cherry Tomatoes • Fresh Fruit Medley • Maple Carrot Cupcakes 33

Deluxe Bacon Burgers • Homemade Potato Salad • Colorful Vegetable Salad • Coffee Ice Cream 35

Spanish Corn with Fish Sticks • Raisin Broccoli Salad • Pudding-Topped Fruit Salad • Lemon Graham Squares....................37

Tangy Pork Barbecue • Apple Iceberg Salad • Crabby Deviled Eggs • Date Bar Dessert..39

Slow-Cooked Orange Chicken • Zesty Broccoli • Oatmeal Yeast Bread • Pineapple Coconut Pie..41

Old-Fashioned Swiss Steak • Baked Carrots • Feather-Light Biscuits • Chef's Salad 43

Oven-Barbecued Spareribs • Salad with Creamy Dressing • Old-Fashioned Baked Beans • Zucchini Cobbler....................45

Pan-Fried Trout • Creamed Sweet Peas • Caraway Rye Bread • Lemon Bars 47

Poor Man's Steak • Scalloped Cheese Potatoes • 12-Hour Salad • Peanutty Pie 49

Crispy Lemon-Fried Chicken • Red Potato Salad • Pennsylvania Dutch Cucumbers • Strawberry Shortcake..................................51

Deviled Corned Beef Buns • Summer Vegetable Salad • Creamy Coleslaw • Banana Cream Dessert..................................53

Arizona Chicken • Vegetable Rice Medley • Chili Cornmeal Crescents • Orange Zucchini Cake 55

Baked Lemon Chicken

This lovely chicken is as good cold as it is right out of the oven. It's moist, tender and lemony with a nice crunch. It's a delicious picnic entree as well as a wonderful meal with scalloped or baked potatoes and a fresh green salad on the side. —Marion Lowery, Medford, Oregon

    3 tablespoons butter *or* margarine, melted
    2 tablespoons lemon juice
    1 garlic clove, minced
    1/2 teaspoon salt
    1/4 teaspoon pepper
    1/2 cup seasoned bread crumbs
    4 boneless skinless chicken breast halves

In a shallow dish, combine the first five ingredients. Place bread crumbs in another dish. Dip chicken in butter mixture, then coat with crumbs.

Place in a greased 13-in. x 9-in. x 2-in. baking pan. Drizzle with remaining butter mixture. Bake, uncovered, at 350° for 25-30 minutes or until juices run clear. **Yield:** 4 servings.

Green Beans with Cherry Tomatoes

I found that beans, basil and tomatoes make a very tasty combination of flavors, especially in summer, when all these ingredients can be garden fresh. I like to serve this pretty vegetable dish when entertaining. It's so colorful! —Shirley Heare, Fayetteville, North Carolina

1-1/2 pounds fresh green beans, cut into 2-inch
        pieces
1-1/2 cups water
    1/4 cup butter *or* margarine
    1 tablespoon sugar
1-1/2 teaspoons dried basil
    1/2 teaspoon garlic salt
    1/4 teaspoon salt
    1/8 teaspoon pepper
    2 cups halved cherry tomatoes
    3 fresh basil leaves

Place beans and water in a saucepan; bring to a boil. Reduce heat; cover and simmer for 12-15 minutes or until crisp-tender.

Meanwhile, melt butter in a skillet; stir in sugar, basil, garlic salt, salt and pepper. Add tomatoes; saute until tender. Drain beans; top with tomato mixture. Garnish with basil. **Yield:** 6-8 servings.

Fresh Fruit Medley

Sweet, light, versatile and good for you all describe this fruit salad. Many combinations of fruit can be used. I've even tossed in chopped lettuce or miniature marshmallows to lure the grandkids! —Patricia Ford
Creve Coeur, Illinois

    1 medium ripe banana, sliced, *divided*
    2 tablespoons mayonnaise

    1 teaspoon sugar
    1 kiwifruit, peeled, sliced and quartered
    1 medium pear, cubed
    1 small apple, cubed
    12 seedless green grapes, halved

In a large bowl, mash half of the banana slices. Stir in mayonnaise and sugar. Add the kiwi, pear, apple, grapes and remaining banana slices; toss gently. Serve immediately. **Yield:** 3-4 servings.

Maple Carrot Cupcakes

I come from a family of cooks and was inspired to cook and bake ever since I was young. Mother and Grandmom were always in the kitchen cooking up something. This recipe is handed down from Grandmom and is always requested at special gatherings. —Lisa Ann DiNunzio, Vineland, New Jersey

    2 cups all-purpose flour
    1 cup sugar
    1 teaspoon baking powder
    1 teaspoon baking soda
    1 teaspoon ground cinnamon
    1/2 teaspoon salt
    4 eggs
    1 cup vegetable oil
    1/2 cup maple syrup
    3 cups grated carrots (about 6 medium)
FROSTING:
    1 package (8 ounces) cream cheese, softened
    1/4 cup butter *or* margarine, softened
    1/4 cup maple syrup
    1 teaspoon vanilla extract
Chopped walnuts, optional

In a large bowl, combine the first six ingredients. In another bowl, beat eggs, oil and syrup. Stir into dry ingredients just until moistened. Fold in carrots.

Fill greased or paper-lined muffin cups two-thirds full. Bake at 350° for 20-25 minutes or until a toothpick comes out clean. Cool for 5 minutes before removing from pans to wire racks.

For frosting, combine the cream cheese, butter, maple syrup and vanilla in a mixing bowl; beat until smooth. Frost the cooled cupcakes. Sprinkle with nuts if desired. **Yield:** 1-1/2 dozen.

Cooking Chicken

Both under- and overcooking result in a tough chicken. For the most tender results, cook boneless skinless chicken breast halves to an internal temperature of 170°. Bone-in chicken parts should read 170° for white meat and 180° for dark meat.

Deluxe Bacon Burgers

I created this recipe and won a red ribbon for it in a 1976 cookbook contest. It's like meat loaf in a bun, so it's very hearty. Sometimes I'll serve it with gravy and without the bun. Either way, it's delicious.
—Bernadine Dirmeyer, Harpster, Ohio

   2 large carrots, grated
   1 large onion, grated
   1 cup mashed potato flakes
   2 eggs, lightly beaten
   1 garlic clove, minced
   1 teaspoon salt
Pepper to taste
   2 pounds ground beef
   8 bacon strips
   8 hamburger buns, optional
   8 lettuce leaves, optional

In a large bowl, combine the first seven ingredients. Crumble beef over mixture and mix gently. Shape into eight patties. Wrap a bacon strip around each patty; secure with toothpicks.

In a large skillet, cook the burgers until the meat is no longer pink and the bacon is crisp. Remove toothpicks. Serve burgers on lettuce-lined buns if desired. **Yield:** 8 servings.

Homemade Potato Salad

My best recipes are from friends and family. This one came from my aunt—I learned to cook by watching and helping her. I have so many family favorites that I created my own cookbook. I print it out, illustrate and annotate it to give new brides. It is always well received and treasured.
—Patty Kile
Greentown, Pennsylvania

   1 tablespoon sugar
   2 teaspoons all-purpose flour
   1/4 teaspoon ground mustard
Pinch salt
   1 egg, beaten
   1/3 cup water
   1 tablespoon vinegar
   3/4 cup mayonnaise or salad dressing
   5 large potatoes, peeled and cubed
   4 hard-cooked eggs, chopped
   1 cup chopped celery
   1/4 cup chopped green onions
Salt and pepper to taste

In a small saucepan, combine the sugar, flour, mustard and salt. Combine egg, water and vinegar; stir into dry ingredients until smooth. Bring to a boil over medium heat, stirring constantly. Cook and stir for 2 minutes. Remove from the heat; cool slightly. Stir in the mayonnaise.

In a bowl, combine the potatoes, hard-cooked eggs, celery, onions, salt and pepper. Add the dressing and toss gently to coat. Refrigerate until serving. **Yield:** 8-10 servings.

Colorful Vegetable Salad

When I had a large vegetable garden, I had fun creating recipes, depending on what was ready for picking. I've found this salad complements meat or fish entrees.
—Mildred Sherrer, Bay City, Texas

   3 cups canned or frozen corn, thawed
   1 can (15 ounces) black beans, rinsed and drained
   3 medium tomatoes, seeded and diced
   1 cup chopped green pepper
   1 cup chopped sweet red pepper
DRESSING:
   1/4 cup olive or vegetable oil
   3 tablespoons lime juice
   2 tablespoons minced fresh cilantro or parsley
   1 garlic clove, minced
   1 teaspoon salt
   1/2 teaspoon pepper

In a large bowl, combine the first five ingredients. In a jar with a tight-fitting lid, combine the dressing ingredients; shake well. Pour over vegetables and toss to coat. Cover and refrigerate for at least 2 hours before serving. **Yield:** 8 servings.

Coffee Ice Cream

I combined two recipes—one for vanilla ice cream and the other for a special coffee sauce—to create this one. I serve it plain, just scooped into a dessert dish, so the mild, creamy coffee flavor can be enjoyed to the fullest.
—Theresa Hansen, Pensacola, Florida

   1/4 cup sugar
   1 tablespoon cornstarch
   1 tablespoon instant coffee granules
   2 tablespoons butter or margarine, melted
   1 cup milk
   1 teaspoon vanilla extract
   1 can (14 ounces) sweetened condensed milk
   2 cups heavy whipping cream

In a saucepan, stir sugar, cornstarch, coffee and butter until blended. Stir in milk. Bring to a boil over medium heat; cook and stir for 2 minutes or until thickened. Remove from the heat; stir in vanilla. Cool completely.

Stir in condensed milk. In a mixing bowl, beat cream until stiff peaks form; fold into milk mixture. Pour into a 9-in. square pan. Cover and freeze for 6 hours or until firm. **Yield:** 1-1/2 quarts.

Ice Cream IQ

Homemade ice cream should be "ripened" in the freezer for at least 4 hours to fully develop its flavor and texture.

Spanish Corn with Fish Sticks

This tasty casserole is a family favorite and is my old standby for social functions. It's easy to assemble and economical, too.   —Roberta Nelson, Portland, Oregon

   1/4 cup chopped onion
   1/4 cup chopped green pepper
   1/4 cup butter *or* margarine
   1/4 cup all-purpose flour
1-1/2 teaspoons salt
   1/4 teaspoon pepper
    2 teaspoons sugar
    2 cans (14-1/2 ounces *each*) stewed tomatoes
    2 packages (10 ounces *each*) frozen corn, partially thawed
    2 packages (12 ounces *each*) frozen fish sticks

In a skillet, saute the onion and green pepper in butter until tender. Stir in the flour, salt, pepper and sugar until blended. Add tomatoes; bring to a boil. Reduce heat; simmer, uncovered, for 3-5 minutes or until thickened, stirring occasionally. Stir in corn.

Transfer to two greased 11-in. x 7-in. x 2-in. baking dishes. Cover and bake at 350° for 25 minutes. Uncover; arrange fish sticks over the top. Bake 15 minutes longer or until fish sticks are heated through. **Yield:** 8-10 servings.

Raisin Broccoli Salad

*Years ago, I needed a colorful dish for my menu and created this salad. I experimented with the dressing until the combination was a success. This is a great make-ahead salad.   —Pat Faircloth
Lillington, North Carolina*

   4 cups broccoli florets
   1 cup chopped green pepper
   1 cup sliced carrots
   1 cup raisins
   1 cup chopped walnuts
   1 medium onion, chopped
   1 cup mayonnaise
1/2 cup sugar
1/4 cup white vinegar

In a large serving bowl, combine the first six ingredients. In a small bowl, combine the mayonnaise, sugar and vinegar until smooth. Pour over vegetable mixture and toss to coat. Cover and refrigerate for at least 1 hour or until serving. **Yield:** 12 servings.

Pudding-Topped Fruit Salad

*My sister shared this recipe with me. She served the fruit in wine goblets, topped with the pudding. For large groups, serve it in a big salad bowl. Either way, it's refreshing and delicious.   —Michelle Masciarelli
Torrington, Connecticut*

   1 can (20 ounces) pineapple chunks
   1 can (8 ounces) crushed pineapple, undrained
   1 cup (8 ounces) sour cream
   1 package (3.4 ounces) instant vanilla pudding mix
   2 medium ripe bananas, sliced
   2 cups fresh *or* frozen blueberries, thawed
   2 medium ripe peaches, peeled and sliced
   2 cups sliced fresh strawberries
   1 cup seedless green grapes
   1 cup seedless red grapes
Fresh mint, optional

Drain pineapple chunks, reserving juice; refrigerate pineapple. Add water to juice if necessary to measure 3/4 cup. In a bowl, combine the juice, crushed pineapple, sour cream and pudding mix until blended. Cover and refrigerate for at least 3 hours.

In a large bowl, combine the bananas, blueberries, peaches, strawberries, grapes and pineapple chunks. Spread pudding mixture over the top. Garnish with mint if desired. **Yield:** 12-14 servings.

Lemon Graham Squares

*My Aunt Jackie brought these lemon bars to every family gathering. They're my favorite lemon dessert. The crispy top and bottom give a nice texture.
—Janis Plourde, Smooth Rock Falls, Ontario*

   1 can (14 ounces) sweetened condensed milk
1/2 cup lemon juice
1-1/2 cups graham cracker crumbs (about 24 squares)
  3/4 cup all-purpose flour
  1/3 cup packed brown sugar
  1/2 teaspoon baking powder
Pinch salt
  1/2 cup butter *or* margarine, melted

In a bowl, combine the milk and lemon juice; mix well and set aside. In another bowl, combine the cracker crumbs, flour, brown sugar, baking powder and salt. Stir in butter until crumbly.

Press half of the crumb mixture into a greased 9-inch square baking dish. Pour lemon mixture over crust; sprinkle with remaining crumbs. Bake at 375° for 20-25 minutes or until lightly browned. Cool on a wire rack. **Yield:** 3 dozen.

Juicing Lemons

Room temperature lemons will yield more juice than those that are refrigerated. Use your palm to roll lemons around on the countertop a few times before squeezing to maximize juice yield.

Tangy Pork Barbecue

A dear neighbor shared this zesty recipe with me in the late '50s—she'd found it in a Marine Officers' Wives cookbook. This barbecue has always been a great hit with my family. —Carmine Walters
San Jose, California

2 tablespoons butter *or* margarine
3 tablespoons all-purpose flour
1 bottle (28 ounces) ketchup
2 cups boiling water
1/4 cup vinegar
1/4 cup Worcestershire sauce
1 medium onion, chopped
1 garlic clove, minced
2 teaspoons chili powder
1 teaspoon salt
1 teaspoon ground mustard
1/8 teaspoon cayenne pepper
1 boneless pork loin roast (3-1/2 to 4 pounds)
12 sandwich buns, split

In a Dutch oven over medium heat, melt the butter. Stir in the flour until smooth. Add the next 10 ingredients; bring to a boil. Add the pork roast. Reduce heat and cover and simmer for 3 hours or until the meat is very tender.

Remove meat; shred with two forks or a pastry blender. Skim fat from cooking juices; return meat to juices and heat through. Serve with a slotted spoon on buns. **Yield:** 12 servings.

Apple Iceberg Salad

I created this recipe when my children were small and fussed about eating fruits and vegetables. The slightly sweet dressing makes it a hit. This salad was part of our Friday meal when I served fried fish and boiled potatoes. My grown children call this "Mom's Salad". —M.J. Zimmerman, Altoona, Pennsylvania

1 cup mayonnaise
1/4 cup sugar
2 tablespoons cider vinegar
2 tablespoons evaporated milk
2 large red apples, diced
1 medium head iceberg lettuce, torn

In a bowl, combine the mayonnaise, sugar, vinegar and milk; mix well. Add apples. Cover and refrigerate for 1 hour. Just before serving, toss with lettuce. **Yield:** 8-10 servings.

Crabby Deviled Eggs

Whenever I serve these eggs, my guests are usually puzzled by the unique taste…it's not the traditional taste of deviled eggs. The surprise ingredient is crabmeat, which makes for a delightful change of pace. —Reginald Davis, Orlando, Florida

12 hard-cooked eggs
1 can (6 ounces) crabmeat, drained, flaked and cartilage removed
1/4 cup mayonnaise *or* salad dressing
2 tablespoons sweet pickle relish
1 tablespoon prepared mustard
2 teaspoons seafood seasoning
1/4 teaspoon pepper

Slice eggs in half lengthwise. Remove yolks and set the whites aside. In a small bowl, mash yolks with a fork. Add crab, mayonnaise, relish, mustard, seafood seasoning and pepper; mix well. Stuff or pipe into egg whites. Refrigerate until serving. **Yield:** 12 servings.

Date Bar Dessert

My mother copied this recipe from a Quaker Oats box in the 1950s, and it remains one of our favorite treats today. I serve these date-filled squares as a snack or for dessert topped with a dollop of whipped cream. —Jill McCon, Montrose, Michigan

1-3/4 cups old-fashioned oats
1-1/2 cups all-purpose flour
1 cup packed brown sugar
1 teaspoon baking soda
1/2 teaspoon salt
1 cup cold butter *or* margarine
2-1/2 cups chopped dates
3/4 cup sugar
3/4 cup water
1/2 cup chopped walnuts
Whipped topping

In a large bowl, combine oats, flour, brown sugar, baking soda and salt. Cut in butter until mixture resembles coarse crumbs. Press into a greased 13-in. x 9-in. x 2-in. baking pan.

In a saucepan, combine the dates, sugar and water. Cook for 10 minutes or until thickened, stirring frequently. Stir in the walnuts. Spread over the crust. Bake at 350° for 30 minutes. Cool on a wire rack. Cut into squares and top with whipped topping. **Yield:** 18 servings.

Pack a Picnic

Cold foods should be kept at 40° or colder. When packing a cooler, it should be about 25% ice and 75% food.

Place ice on the bottom and along the sides of the cooler. Then place the heaviest and most perishable foods on top of the ice. Fill in with lighter items.

Consider packing two containers—a picnic basket for tableware and nonperishable items and a cooler for cold food and beverages.

Slow-Cooked Orange Chicken

Everyone likes the taste of this dish, including my grandchildren. A hint of orange gives the chicken a delicious flavor. This is a favorite of mine. It travels well, and I often take it to potluck suppers. —Nancy Wit
Fremont, Nebraska

- 1 broiler-fryer chicken (3 pounds), cut up and skin removed
- 3 cups orange juice
- 1 cup chopped celery
- 1 cup chopped green pepper
- 1 can (4 ounces) mushroom stems and pieces, drained
- 4 teaspoons dried minced onion
- 1 tablespoon minced fresh parsley *or* 1 teaspoon dried parsley flakes
- 1/2 teaspoon salt
- 1/4 teaspoon pepper
- 3 tablespoons cornstarch
- 3 tablespoons cold water
Hot cooked rice

Combine the first nine ingredients in a slow cooker. Cover and cook on low for 4 hours or until meat juices run clear. Combine the cornstarch and cold water until smooth; stir into the cooking juices. Cover and cook on high for 30-45 minutes or until thickened. Serve over rice. **Yield:** 4 servings.

Zesty Broccoli

I've been a vegetarian for over 20 years and often experiment with flavors compatible to the many vegetables I prepare. My nephew, who lived with me a year while going to graduate school, thought this was one of my best creations. It's not only beautiful, it's delicious and nutritious, too. —Louiza Kemyan
Palm Springs, California

- 4 cups broccoli florets
- 1/4 cup water
- 2 teaspoons olive *or* vegetable oil
- 1 to 2 garlic cloves, minced
- 1/2 teaspoon salt
Dash crushed red pepper flakes

In a saucepan, combine the first five ingredients; bring to a boil. Reduce heat; cover and simmer until broccoli is crisp-tender, about 5 minutes. Drain; add red pepper flakes and toss. **Yield:** 4 servings.

Oatmeal Yeast Bread

When this old-fashioned bread is baking, it reminds me of childhood and the warm, inviting aromas that greeted me when I got home from school. The light sweet flavor, crispy crust and hearty texture of this bread made for a special treat when Mom baked it for us.
—Gloria Murtha, West Mifflin, Pennsylvania

- 1 can (12 ounces) evaporated milk
- 1/2 cup water

- 2 tablespoons shortening
- 2 cups plus 2 teaspoons old-fashioned oats, *divided*
- 1/3 cup packed brown sugar
- 1-1/2 teaspoons salt
- 1 package (1/4 ounce) active dry yeast
- 1 cup warm water (110° to 115°)
- 5 to 5-1/2 cups all-purpose flour
- 1 egg, beaten

In a saucepan over medium heat, bring the milk, water and shortening to a boil. Meanwhile, combine 2 cups oats, brown sugar and salt in a mixing bowl. Add the milk mixture; let stand until mixture reaches 110°-115°. In a small bowl, dissolve yeast in warm water; add to oat mixture. Add 3 cups flour; beat until smooth. Add enough remaining flour to form a soft dough.

Turn onto a floured surface; knead until smooth and elastic, about 6-8 minutes. Place in a greased bowl, turning once to grease top. Cover and let rise in a warm place until doubled, about 1 hour.

Punch dough down; divide in half. Shape into two loaves; transfer to greased 8-in. x 4-in. x 2-in. loaf pans. Cover and let rise until doubled, about 40 minutes. Brush with egg; sprinkle with remaining oats. Bake at 350° for 35-40 minutes or until golden. Remove from pans and cool on wire racks. **Yield:** 2 loaves.

Pineapple Coconut Pie

My daughter introduced me to several recipes that are low in sugar after I found out I have diabetes. This was one of them, and it's become one of my favorite desserts. It's quick and easy to make, too. —Elsie Wilson
Freeman, Missouri

- 1 cup cold milk
- 1 package (3.4 ounces) sugar-free instant vanilla pudding mix
- 1/2 cup flaked coconut
- 1 can (8 ounces) crushed unsweetened pineapple, drained
- 1 pastry shell (9 inches), baked
Whipped topping

In a mixing bowl, beat milk and pudding mix until thickened. Stir in the coconut and pineapple. Pour into pastry shell. Chill for at least 2 hours. Garnish with whipped topping. **Yield:** 8 servings.

No Peeking!

Refrain from lifting the lid while the slow cooker is cooking. The loss of steam can mean an additional 15 to 30 minutes of cooking each time you lift the lid.

Old-Fashioned Swiss Steak

Our kids come to visit us often, and they always request this Swiss steak. The kids enjoy it so much, they look forward to leftovers the next day. —*Eleanore Hill*
Fresno, California

1/2 cup plus 2 tablespoons all-purpose flour, *divided*
2 teaspoons salt, *divided*
3/4 teaspoon pepper, *divided*
1/2 teaspoon garlic salt
2 pounds boneless round steak, cut into serving-size pieces
3 tablespoons vegetable oil
1 garlic clove, minced
2 cups chopped green pepper
1 cup chopped celery
1 cup chopped onion
2 cans (14-1/2 ounces *each*) diced tomatoes, undrained
1 cup beef broth
1 tablespoon soy sauce
1/4 cup cold water

In a large plastic bag, combine 1/2 cup flour, 1 teaspoon salt, 1/2 teaspoon pepper and garlic salt. Add beef and toss to coat. Remove meat from bag and pound with a mallet to tenderize.

Heat oil in a Dutch oven; brown the meat. Add garlic, green pepper, celery and onion; cook and stir for 10 minutes. Add tomatoes, broth, soy sauce and remaining salt and pepper. Cover and bake at 325° for 2 hours.

Remove from the oven and return to stovetop. In a small bowl, combine water and remaining flour; stir into juices. Bring to a boil over medium heat, stirring constantly until thickened. **Yield:** 6-8 servings.

Baked Carrots

These carrots are compatible with most any meal. The chicken broth gives them great flavor. For a variation, this vegetable combination is delicious mashed in with potatoes. . —*Eleanore Hill*

1 pound carrots, cut into sticks
1 bunch green onions with tops, chopped
1 cup chicken broth

Place the carrots and onions in an ungreased 1-qt. baking dish; pour chicken broth over all. Cover and bake at 325° for 1 hour. **Yield:** 6 servings.

Feather-Light Biscuits

I usually use a glass or baking powder can lid as a cutter so these biscuits will be bigger than average size...and I always bake some extras to send home with the kids. They liked to split them and fill them with cheese or peanut butter and strawberry jam.
—*Eleanore Hill*

6 cups biscuit/baking mix
1/4 cup sugar
1 package (1/4 ounce) active dry yeast
1/3 cup shortening
1 to 1-1/4 cups warm water (120° to 130°)
1/4 cup butter *or* margarine, melted

In a large bowl, combine the baking mix, sugar and yeast. Cut in shortening until mixture resembles coarse crumbs. Stir in enough warm water to make a soft and slightly sticky dough.

Turn onto a floured surface; knead gently 3-4 times. Roll dough to 3/4-in. thickness; cut with a 2-1/2-in. round biscuit cutter. Place on ungreased baking sheets. Brush tops with melted butter. Bake at 400° for 10-12 minutes or until lightly browned. **Yield:** about 2 dozen.

Chef's Salad

At the restaurant my husband and I used to own, we always made three dressings to go with this salad...blue cheese, French and Thousand Island. At home, I serve all three dressings, too, because everyone has their favorite. Sometimes the kids use a tablespoon of each.
—*Eleanore Hill*

1/2 head iceberg lettuce, torn
1 can (15 ounces) garbanzo beans, rinsed and drained, optional
1 small red onion, chopped
1/2 cup sliced radishes
1 small cucumber, chopped
1 small tomato, chopped
1 cup julienned fully cooked ham
1 cup julienned Swiss *or* cheddar cheese
DRESSING:
1 cup salad dressing *or* mayonnaise
1/2 cup *each* ketchup, sweet pickle relish and chopped onion
Dash garlic salt

In a large salad bowl, combine lettuce, beans if desired, onion, radishes, cucumber and tomato. Arrange ham and cheese on top. Cover and refrigerate until serving.

In a small bowl, combine all dressing ingredients; stir until well blended. Chill for 1 hour. Serve with the salad. **Yield:** 6 servings.

Better Biscuits

For the flakiest biscuits, use a pastry blender or fork to thoroughly cut shortening into the dry ingredients. Don't overmix or overknead the dough. Dip the biscuit cutter into flour after each cut to prevent sticking. Press the floured cutter into the dough and lift straight up; don't twist it.

Oven-Barbecued Spareribs

One of my family's favorites, this dish is often at the heart of our special meals. All our married children live nearby, so we have family gatherings often. Whenever I prepare these spareribs, I need a large quantity—most everyone asks for seconds. —LaVerna Mjones
Moorhead, Minnesota

- 6 pounds pork spareribs
- 3 cups ketchup
- 1-1/2 cups packed brown sugar
- 3/4 cup chopped onion
- 1 teaspoon garlic powder
- 4 to 5 teaspoons liquid smoke, optional

Cut ribs into serving-size pieces; place with bone side down on a rack in a shallow roasting pan. Bake, uncovered, at 350° for 30 minutes.

Meanwhile, in a medium saucepan, combine remaining ingredients; simmer, uncovered, for 20 minutes, stirring occasionally. Drain ribs; pour sauce over all.

Cover and bake for 30-40 minutes or until tender. Uncover; bake 30 minutes longer, brushing several times with sauce. **Yield:** 6-8 servings.

Salad with Creamy Dressing

I like to make this salad in the early growing season when all the greens are tender and fresh. When our children were growing up, our vegetable garden was always bountiful. Many of the dishes I prepared came right from the garden. —Beth Miller, Ocala, Florida

- 2/3 cup sour cream
- 2/3 cup mayonnaise *or* salad dressing
- 2/3 cup milk
- 2-1/2 teaspoons sugar
- 1-1/4 teaspoons prepared mustard
- 3/4 teaspoon garlic powder
- 3/4 teaspoon lemon-pepper seasoning
- 1 large head iceberg lettuce, torn
- 2 to 3 cups torn fresh spinach
- 1 small onion, sliced
- 1 large tomato, cut into wedges
- 1 medium green pepper, julienned
- 1 cup seasoned croutons

In a small bowl, combine the first seven ingredients and whisk until smooth. Cover and refrigerate for at least 1 hour.

In a large salad bowl, combine the lettuce, spinach, onion, tomato, green pepper and croutons. Add the dressing and toss; serve immediately. **Yield:** 12-16 servings.

Old-Fashioned Baked Beans

These savory beans were a specialty my dear grandma frequently prepared. When I even think of this dish, I can smell the enticing aroma that met us at the door when we went over to Grandma's for Sunday dinner. Every dish she made was a labor of love.
—Marjorie Thompson, West Sacramento, California

- 1 pound dry great northern beans
- 2 quarts water, *divided*
- 1/2 teaspoon salt
- 1 medium onion, chopped
- 2 tablespoons prepared mustard
- 2 tablespoons brown sugar
- 2 tablespoons dark molasses
- 1/2 pound sliced bacon, cooked and crumbled

Place beans and 1 qt. water in a saucepan; bring to a boil. Boil for 2 minutes. Remove from the heat; cover and let stand for 1 hour.

Drain and rinse; return beans to saucepan. Add salt and remaining water; bring to a boil. Reduce heat; cover and simmer for 1 to 1-1/4 hours or until the beans are tender. Drain, reserving 2 cups cooking liquid.

In a greased 13-in. x 9-in. x 2-in. baking dish, combine beans, onion, mustard, brown sugar, molasses, bacon and 1 cup of reserved cooking liquid. Cover and bake at 400° for 45 minutes or until the beans have reached desired thickness, stirring occasionally (add additional reserved cooking liquid if needed). **Yield:** 12-16 servings.

Zucchini Cobbler

This is my surprise dessert! No one ever guesses that the secret ingredient is zucchini. Everyone says it tastes like apples. This cobbler is a great dessert to make for a potluck supper or to serve a crowd. It's been requested time and again in my house, and I'm always happy to make it. —Joanne Fazio, Carbondale, Pennsylvania

- 8 cups chopped seeded peeled zucchini (about 3 pounds)
- 2/3 cup lemon juice
- 1 cup sugar
- 1 teaspoon ground cinnamon
- 1/2 teaspoon ground nutmeg

CRUST:
- 4 cups all-purpose flour
- 2 cups sugar
- 1-1/2 cups cold butter *or* margarine
- 1 teaspoon ground cinnamon

In a large saucepan over medium-low heat, cook and stir zucchini and lemon juice for 15-20 minutes or until zucchini is tender. Add sugar, cinnamon and nutmeg; simmer 1 minute longer. Remove from the heat; set aside.

For crust, combine the flour and sugar in a bowl; cut in butter until the mixture resembles coarse crumbs. Stir 1/2 cup into zucchini mixture. Press half of remaining crust mixture into a greased 15-in. x 10-in. x 1-in. baking pan.

Spread zucchini over top; crumble remaining crust mixture over zucchini. Sprinkle with cinnamon. Bake at 375° for 35-40 minutes or until golden and bubbly. **Yield:** 16-20 servings.

Pan-Fried Trout

One summer when my husband and I were enjoying our first getaway in years, we found ourselves stranded in our cabin cruiser with a dead battery. When hunger set in, my husband rigged up a fishing line, and soon there were two trout sizzling on the portable grill. We eventually made it home all right…and kept the recipe we'd devised. —Felicia Cummings, Raymond, Maine

    4 lake trout fillets (about 8 ounces *each*)
1/2 cup grated Parmesan cheese
1/2 cup bacon-flavored crackers, crushed
1/2 cup cornmeal
1/4 to 1/2 teaspoon garlic salt
Pinch pepper
    2 eggs
1/2 cup milk
1/2 cup vegetable oil
Lemon wedges *and/or* snipped fresh chives *or* parsley, optional

Rinse fish in cold water; pat dry. In a shallow bowl, combine the cheese, cracker crumbs, cornmeal, garlic salt and pepper. In another bowl, beat eggs and milk.

Dip the fish in the egg mixture, then gently roll in the crumb mixture. In a skillet, fry the fish in oil for 5-7 minutes or until it flakes easily with a fork, turning once. If desired, garnish with lemon, chives and/or parsley. **Yield:** 4 servings.

Creamed Sweet Peas

Mom's garden in the '40s provided us with many delicious vegetables, but her sweet peas were the best. She would pick them fresh, shell them and fix the best creamed sweet peas ever on her huge wood stove.
—Jean Patten, Pineville, Louisiana

    1 tablespoon all-purpose flour
1/4 cup sugar
2/3 cup milk
    2 cups fresh sweet peas *or* 1 package (10 ounces) frozen peas, thawed
1/4 teaspoon pepper

In a medium saucepan, combine flour, sugar and milk; mix well. Add the peas and pepper; bring to a boil. Reduce heat; simmer for 10-12 minutes or until the peas are heated through and the sauce has thickened. **Yield:** 4 servings.

Caraway Rye Bread

It was probably 45 years ago when the thrashers came to dinner at our house and Mother served this bread. Today, every time I bake it, I get nostalgic for those days. My parents were emigrants from Czechoslovakia and couldn't speak English very well. The thrashers hardly talked anyway—they were too busy enjoying Mother's delicious food! —Millie Feather, Baroda, Michigan

    2 packages (1/4 ounce *each*) active dry yeast
    2 cups warm water (110° to 115°), *divided*
1/4 cup packed brown sugar
    1 tablespoon caraway seed
    1 tablespoon vegetable oil
    2 teaspoons salt
2-1/2 cups rye flour
2-3/4 to 3-1/4 cups all-purpose flour

In a large mixing bowl, dissolve yeast in 1/2 cup warm water. Add brown sugar, caraway, oil, salt and remaining water; mix well. Stir in rye flour and 1 cup all-purpose flour; beat until smooth. Add enough remaining all-purpose flour to form a soft dough.

Turn onto a floured surface; knead until smooth and elastic, about 6-8 minutes. Place in a greased bowl, turning once to grease top. Cover and let rise in a warm place until doubled, about 1 hour.

Punch dough down; divide in half. Shape each half into a ball; place in two greased 8-in. round baking pans. Flatten balls to a 6-in. diameter. Cover and let rise until nearly doubled, about 30 minutes. Bake at 375° for 25-30 minutes or until golden brown. **Yield:** 2 loaves.

Lemon Bars

This dessert is a delightful recipe from my mother's file. I've been serving it for many years. The bars have a wonderful tangy flavor, and they're always a hit. For variety of color and shape, they're a nice addition to a platter of cookies. —Etta Soucy, Mesa, Arizona

    1 cup all-purpose flour
1/2 cup butter *or* margarine, softened
1/4 cup confectioners' sugar
FILLING:
    2 eggs
    1 cup sugar
    2 tablespoons all-purpose flour
1/2 teaspoon baking powder
    2 tablespoons lemon juice
    1 teaspoon grated lemon peel
Additional confectioners' sugar

Combine the first three ingredients; pat into an ungreased 8-in. square baking pan. Bake at 350° for 20 minutes. Meanwhile, beat eggs in a mixing bowl. Add sugar, flour, baking powder, lemon juice and peel; beat until frothy. Pour over the crust. Bake at 350° for 25 minutes or until light golden brown. Cool. Dust with confectioners' sugar. **Yield:** 9 servings.

Pea Particulars

Peas should be crisp-tender when cooked. Overdone peas will lose their bright-green color and much of their fresh flavor.

Poor Man's Steak

On a pastor's budget and with seven young children, we didn't have steak very often. But we were just as satisfied with this wonderful dish Mom dreamed up—a country-style "steak" with creamy gravy. —Dorothy Bowen
Thomasville, North Carolina

    1 cup water
    1 cup cracker crumbs
    1 teaspoon salt
    3 pounds ground beef
All-purpose flour
    2 to 3 tablespoons vegetable oil
    1 can (10-3/4 ounces) condensed cream of
       mushroom soup, undiluted

In a large bowl, combine water, cracker crumbs and salt; add beef and mix well. Press into a 15-in. x 10-in. x 1-in. baking pan lined with waxed paper. Cover and refrigerate overnight.

Cut the meat into 12 squares. Coat each square lightly with flour; brown in oil in a skillet, a few pieces at a time. Drain.

Remove waxed paper from the baking pan; spread the soup in bottom of pan. Place meat squares in a single layer over soup. Bake, uncovered, at 300° for 35-40 minutes. To serve, spoon some soup over each meat square. **Yield:** 12 servings.

Scalloped Cheese Potatoes

Mom decided to devise her own recipe for scalloped potatoes, and she cooked up a winner with this one. There was never a morsel left in the serving dish! The flavor of mushrooms gives the potatoes a unique taste.
—Dorothy Bowen

    4 pounds potatoes, peeled and thinly sliced
    2 cans (10-3/4 ounces *each*) condensed cream
       of mushroom soup, undiluted
    1/4 cup butter *or* margarine, *divided*
    2 cups (8 ounces) shredded sharp cheddar
       cheese, *divided*

In a large bowl, combine potatoes and soup. Layer half of the mixture in a greased 13-in. x 9-in. x 2-in. baking dish. Dot with half of the butter and sprinkle with half of the cheese. Repeat layers. Bake, uncovered, at 350° for 60-70 minutes or until the potatoes are tender. **Yield:** 12 servings.

12-Hour Salad

This recipe was Mom's scrumptious scheme to get her kids to eat vegetables. She never had any trouble when she served this colorful crunchy salad. Mom thought this salad was a real bonus for the cook since it must be made the night before. —Dorothy Bowen

    8 cups torn salad greens
1-1/2 cups chopped celery

    2 medium green peppers, chopped
    1 medium red onion, chopped
    1 package (10 ounces) frozen peas, thawed
    1 cup salad dressing *or* mayonnaise
    1 cup (8 ounces) sour cream
    3 tablespoons sugar
    1 cup (4 ounces) shredded cheddar cheese
    1/2 pound sliced bacon, cooked and crumbled

Place salad greens in the bottom of a 3-qt. bowl or 13-in. x 9-in. x 2-in. dish. Top with layers of celery, green peppers, onion and peas; do not toss. Combine salad dressing, sour cream and sugar; spread over salad. Sprinkle with cheese and bacon. Cover and refrigerate overnight. **Yield:** 12 servings.

Peanutty Pie

Through the years, Mom has probably made thousands of these pies for family and friends. The combination of peanut butter, cream cheese and chocolate in a deliciously tender pie crust is a delightful finale to any meal. —Dorothy Bowen

    3/4 cup creamy peanut butter
    1 package (16 ounces) confectioners' sugar
    1 package (8 ounces) cream cheese, softened
    1/3 cup half-and-half cream
    1 carton (16 ounces) frozen whipped topping,
       thawed, *divided*
    2 pastry shells (9 inches *each*), baked
TOPPING:
    1 cup (6 ounces) semisweet chocolate chips
    1/2 cup butter *or* margarine
    3 tablespoons sugar
    1/3 cup half-and-half cream
    1 teaspoon vanilla extract
Chopped peanuts, optional

In a mixing bowl, beat peanut butter, confectioners' sugar, cream cheese and cream until smooth. Add a third of the whipped topping; blend thoroughly. Fold in the remaining whipped topping. Divide and spoon into pastry shells, mounding slightly at edges. Chill.

For topping, heat chocolate chips, butter, sugar and cream in a small saucepan until chips are melted. Remove from heat and add vanilla. Cover and let stand until cool.

Spread over tops of pies to within 1 in. of crust. If desired, sprinkle with peanuts. Chill 4 hours before serving. Refrigerate leftovers. **Yield:** 12-16 servings.

About Peanut Butter

Unopened, peanut butter can be stored in a cool dry place for up to 1 year. Once opened, it will stay fresh for about 3 months.

Crispy Lemon-Fried Chicken

This is my husband's favorite chicken. He loves it done very crispy and well browned. The steps of soaking the chicken pieces in salted lemony water and re-crisping are the secrets. —Shirley Helfenbein, Lapeer, Michigan

> 2 broiler-fryer chickens (2 to 3 pounds *each*),
>   cut up *or* 16 pieces of chicken
> 3-1/2 teaspoons salt, *divided*
> Juice of 1 medium lemon
>   1 cup all-purpose flour
>   1 teaspoon paprika
>   1/8 teaspoon pepper
> Vegetable oil
>   2 tablespoons hot water

Place chicken pieces in a large bowl; add 3 teaspoons of salt, lemon juice and enough water to cover chicken. Soak in refrigerator overnight. Drain thoroughly.

In a paper bag, combine flour, paprika, pepper and remaining salt. Toss chicken pieces in flour mixture; shake off excess.

Heat about 1/2 in. of oil in a large skillet. When hot, carefully add chicken and brown lightly on all sides, about 20 minutes. Reduce heat. Carefully add water; cover and cook until tender, about 20 minutes. Uncover and cook until chicken is crisp, about 10 minutes. **Yield:** 6-8 servings.

Red Potato Salad

I remember digging small red potatoes from the soft warm soil, then gently pushing the plants back into the ground and reminding them to keep on making more potatoes. The new potatoes we brought home were either creamed with peas or made into this fresh salad.
—Shirley Helfenbein

> 3/4 cup sour cream
> 1/2 cup mayonnaise *or* salad dressing
>   2 tablespoons herb *or* white vinegar
> 1-1/2 teaspoons salt
>   1 teaspoon celery seed
>   6 medium red potatoes (about 2 pounds),
>   peeled, cooked and cubed
> 3/4 cup sliced green onions
> 1/3 cup radish slices
> 1/4 cup chopped celery
>   3 to 4 hard-cooked eggs, chopped

In a small bowl, combine sour cream, mayonnaise, vinegar, salt and celery seed; set aside. In a large bowl, combine potatoes, green onions, radishes, celery and eggs. Add dressing and toss lightly. Cover and chill. **Yield:** 6-8 servings.

Pennsylvania Dutch Cucumbers

My mom's side of the family was German and Irish. Settling in Pennsylvania, they adopted some of the cooking and customs of the Pennsylvania Dutch. This is a Dutch dish Mom loved, and today it's my favorite garden salad...the blend of crisp cucumbers and homegrown tomatoes is wonderful! —Shirley Helfenbein

> 3 to 4 small cucumbers
>   1 teaspoon salt
>   1 medium onion, thinly sliced into rings
> 1/2 cup sour cream
>   2 tablespoons vinegar
>   1 tablespoon chopped fresh chives
> 1/2 teaspoon dried dill seed
> 1/4 teaspoon pepper
> Pinch sugar
> Lettuce leaves, optional
> Sliced tomatoes, optional

Peel cucumbers; slice paper-thin into a bowl. Sprinkle with salt; cover and refrigerate for 3-4 hours. Rinse and drain cucumbers. Pat gently to press out excess liquid. Combine cucumbers and onion in a bowl; set aside.

In a small bowl, combine sour cream, vinegar, chives, dill seed, pepper and sugar. Just before serving, add dressing to cucumbers and toss. If desired, arrange lettuce and tomatoes in a serving bowl and spoon cucumbers into the middle. **Yield:** 6 servings.

Strawberry Shortcake

I can still taste the sweet juicy berries piled over warm biscuits and topped with a huge dollop of fresh whipped cream. My father added even more indulgence to this strawberry dessert by first buttering his biscuits.
—Shirley Helfenbein

> 2 cups all-purpose flour
> 2 tablespoons sugar
> 1 tablespoon baking powder
> 1/2 teaspoon salt
> 1/2 cup cold butter *or* margarine
>   1 egg, beaten
> 2/3 cup half-and-half cream
>   1 cup heavy whipping cream
>   2 tablespoons confectioners' sugar
> 1/8 teaspoon vanilla extract
> Additional butter *or* margarine
> 1-1/2 quarts fresh strawberries, sliced

In a bowl, combine flour, sugar, baking powder and salt. Cut in butter until mixture resembles coarse crumbs. In a small bowl, combine egg and half-and-half; add all at once to the crumb mixture and stir just until moistened. Spread batter into a greased 8-in. round baking pan, slightly building up around the edges. Bake at 450° for 16-18 minutes or until golden brown. Remove from pan and cool on a wire rack.

In a mixing bowl, beat whipping cream, confectioners' sugar and vanilla until soft peaks form; set aside. Just before serving, split cake crosswise in half; butter bottom layer. Spoon half of the strawberries over bottom layer. Spread with some of the whipped cream. Cover with top cake layer. Top with remaining berries and whipped cream. Cut into wedges. **Yield:** 6-8 servings.

Deviled Corned Beef Buns

This is quite an old recipe that I've used for years. I've always thought of it as a good "living room picnic" because each sandwich is wrapped individually, making them easy to eat. The sandwich spread keeps for days in the refrigerator, so it's a good thing to have on hand for a quick and easy meal.
—Helen Kennedy
Hudson, New York

1 cup crumbled canned corned beef
1/2 cup shredded process American cheese
1/3 cup chopped stuffed olives
1/3 cup ketchup
2 tablespoons finely chopped green onions
1 tablespoon finely chopped green pepper
1 tablespoon Worcestershire sauce
1/4 teaspoon pepper
4 submarine *or* hoagie rolls, split

In a medium bowl, combine the first eight ingredients. Divide the mixture and spoon onto the bottom of the rolls. Replace the roll tops; wrap each sandwich tightly in foil. Bake at 325° for 20 minutes or until heated through. **Yield:** 4 servings.

Summer Vegetable Salad

This salad is not only delicious, it helped our family weather the Depression. I still remember lining up with Papa to receive dried beans and a 10-pound sack of yellow cornmeal. We used the cornmeal to make polenta. Mother made this salad with vegetables from the garden, and it really tasted good with the polenta.
—Rudy Mancini, Calistoga, California

1/2 cup red wine vinegar *or* cider vinegar
1/3 cup vegetable oil
3 garlic cloves, minced
1/2 teaspoon salt
1/8 teaspoon pepper
1 teaspoon sugar, optional
1/2 pint cherry tomatoes, halved
1 small cucumber, peeled and thinly sliced
1 small green pepper, julienned
1 small red onion, sliced and separated into rings
1 tablespoon chopped fresh basil *or* 1 teaspoon dried basil

In a large bowl, combine the vinegar, oil, garlic, salt, pepper and sugar if desired; mix well. Add the cherry tomatoes, cucumber, green pepper, red onion and basil and toss gently. Cover and chill for at least 1 hour before serving. **Yield:** 4-6 servings.

Creamy Coleslaw

When I was growing up, this was one of our favorite summer salads. I have fond memories of my barefooted sister and me going out to the garden after a cool summer rain to pick the cabbage from our patch. You

might think the ice cream is a strange ingredient, but it makes it extra creamy and adds just a touch of sweetness.
—Mattie Green, Ackley, Iowa

1/2 cup vanilla ice cream, softened
1/4 cup mayonnaise *or* salad dressing
1 teaspoon prepared mustard
1/4 teaspoon salt
Dash pepper
2 cups shredded green cabbage
1 cup shredded red cabbage
1 medium carrot, shredded

In a large bowl, combine ice cream, mayonnaise, mustard, salt and pepper until smooth. Add cabbage and carrot; mix well. Cover and chill for at least 1 hour before serving. **Yield:** 4 servings.

Banana Cream Dessert

When our daughter was at Lehigh University, the school held a recipe contest for "old home-cooking" dishes. Tamie's meal won, and this recipe was part of the menu. For her prize, she was served her dinner in the university's Presidential Dining Room with five of her friends. It was an evening she'll always remember.
—Nancy Walters, Ft. Myers, Florida

1 cup heavy whipping cream
1 teaspoon vanilla extract
1 cup crushed peanut brittle, *divided*
2 ripe bananas, sliced
4 to 6 maraschino cherries

In a mixing bowl, beat cream until soft peaks form. Add vanilla and continue beating just until stiff peaks form. Fold in 3/4 cup peanut brittle and the bananas. Spoon into individual dessert dishes. Chill for 1 hour. Sprinkle with remaining peanut brittle and top each with a cherry. **Yield:** 4-6 servings.

Super Salads

The best salad is a study in contrast and balance of textures, colors and flavors. Mix crunchy ingredients with those that are soft, tangy flavors with mild or slightly sweet, and bright colors with those more muted. The result will be eye-pleasing, palate-teasing and downright delicious.

Salads don't have to consist of greens. There are dozens of fresh vegetables that you can make a salad with, including broccoli, cauliflower, corn, cucumbers, green beans and turnips. Simply peel if necessary, and dice, chop or shred.

Don't overdress salads. Too much dressing will weigh down the ingredients and mask their flavor.

Arizona Chicken

I have a large collection of recipes with a Southwest flavor. Served with either pasta or rice, this is one of my husband's favorites. The moist, flavorful chicken suits any occasion. —Carolyn Deming, Miami, Arizona

        6 boneless skinless chicken breast halves
    1/4 cup vegetable oil, *divided*
        1 medium onion, sliced
        4 cups chopped fresh tomatoes
        2 celery ribs, sliced
    1/4 cup water
    1/4 cup sliced stuffed olives
        2 teaspoons garlic powder
        2 teaspoons dried oregano
        1 teaspoon salt
    1/4 teaspoon pepper
    1/2 pound fresh mushrooms, sliced

In a skillet, brown chicken on both sides in 2 tablespoons oil. Remove and set aside. In same skillet, saute onion in remaining oil until tender. Add tomatoes, celery, water, olives, garlic powder, oregano, salt and pepper; bring to a boil. Cover and simmer for 15 minutes.

Return chicken to pan. Simmer, uncovered, for 15 minutes. Add mushrooms; simmer 15 minutes longer or until meat juices run clear. **Yield:** 6 servings.

Vegetable Rice Medley

When my menu features poultry, I reach for this side dish recipe with its subtle sage flavor. The zesty onion and crunchy celery make a superb combination, and it's easy to make. —Estelle Stimel, Conway, Arkansas

        1 cup chopped onion
        1 cup chopped celery
        1 cup sliced fresh mushrooms
    1/2 cup chopped green pepper
    1/4 cup butter *or* margarine
    2-1/2 cups cooked rice
    3/4 teaspoon salt
    1/2 teaspoon rubbed sage
Pinch pepper

In a large skillet, saute onion, celery, mushrooms and green pepper in butter until tender, about 8 minutes. Stir in the rice, salt, sage and pepper; reduce heat to low. Cook and stir 3-4 minutes longer or until heated through. **Yield:** 6 servings.

Chili Cornmeal Crescents

These unique rolls are tender, light and delicious, with a bit of chili tang. For a fun change of pace, I'll sometimes use blue cornmeal when I make these.
—Marion Lowery, Medford, Oregon

        1 package (1/4 ounce) active dry yeast
    1-3/4 cups warm water (110° to 115°)
        1 egg
        2 tablespoons olive *or* vegetable oil
    1-1/2 cups cornmeal
    1/3 cup sugar
        1 tablespoon chili powder
        1 teaspoon salt
        4 to 4-1/2 cups all-purpose flour

In a small bowl, dissolve yeast in water. In a mixing bowl, beat egg and oil. Add cornmeal, sugar, chili powder, salt, yeast mixture and 2 cups flour; mix well. Add enough remaining flour to form a soft dough.

Turn onto a floured surface; knead until smooth and elastic, about 6-8 minutes. Place in a greased bowl, turning once to grease top. Cover and let rise in a warm place until doubled, about 1 hour.

Punch dough down; divide in half. Roll each portion into a 12-in. circle. Cut into 12 wedges. Roll up each wedge, starting with wide end. Place on greased baking sheets; curve into a crescent shape. Cover and let rise until doubled, about 30 minutes. Bake at 375° for about 20 minutes or until browned. Cool on wire racks. **Yield:** 2 dozen.

Orange Zucchini Cake

I came up with this recipe one year to accommodate our zucchini crop. I used a carrot cake recipe and experimented until I got it right. It's a lovely cake with a tangy orange flavor. —Anne MacDonald, Alma, Quebec

    1/2 cup golden raisins
        1 cup boiling water
    3/4 cup sugar
    1/2 cup vegetable oil
        2 eggs
    1/2 cup All-Bran cereal
    1-1/2 teaspoons grated orange peel
        1 teaspoon vanilla extract
        1 cup all-purpose flour
        1 teaspoon baking powder
        1 teaspoon ground cinnamon
    1/2 teaspoon baking soda
    1/2 teaspoon ground nutmeg
    1/4 teaspoon salt
        1 cup thinly shredded zucchini
FROSTING:
        1 package (3 ounces) cream cheese, softened
        1 tablespoon butter *or* margarine, softened
        1 teaspoon grated orange peel
    1-1/2 cups confectioners' sugar
    1/2 to 1 teaspoon water

Place raisins and water in a bowl; let stand for 5 minutes. Drain; set raisins aside. In a mixing bowl, combine sugar, oil and eggs; mix well. Stir in cereal, orange peel and vanilla. Combine dry ingredients; add to sugar mixture. Mix well. Stir in zucchini and raisins. Pour into a greased 11-in. x 7-in. x 2-in. baking pan. Bake at 325° for 30-35 minutes or until a toothpick inserted near the center comes out clean. Cool.

In a mixing bowl, beat cream cheese, butter and orange peel until light and fluffy. Gradually add sugar and water; beat until smooth. Frost cooled cake. Refrigerate leftovers. **Yield:** 8-10 servings.

pp. 62-63

pp. 60-61

pp. 64-65

pp. 80-81

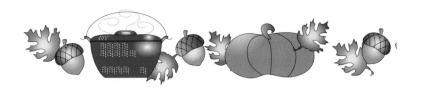

Fall Meals

Autumn Vegetable Beef Stew • Lemony Marinated Vegetables • Crusty Rolls • Country Plum Crumble 59

Turkey with Corn-Bread Dressing • Creamy Broccoli Casserole • Apricot Salad • Harvest Sweet Potato Pie 61

Herbed Pork Roast • Onion Pie • Spinach Pecan Bake • Chewy Ginger Drop Cookies ...63

Sicilian Meat Roll • Parmesan Noodles • Three-Step Salad • Pull-Apart Herb Bread 65

Oven Chicken Stew • Sweet Potato Casserole • Green Beans with Zucchini • Pumpkin Bread Ring...................................67

Barbecued Round Steak • Baked Calico Rice • Favorite Cabbage Salad • Apple Walnut Squares...................................69

Salmon Cakes • Stovetop Macaroni and Cheese • Creamed Peas • Cornmeal Pie........71

Cider-Roasted Chicken • Cinnamon Apple Salad • Butternut Squash Bisque • Pumpkin Custard 73

Spiced Pot Roast • Grandma's Apples and Rice • Turnip Souffle • Baking Powder Biscuits 75

Stuffed Turkey Roll • Peppered Green Beans • Louisiana Sweet Potato Casserole • Berry Cheesecake Parfaits...77

Sauerbraten • Sweet-and-Sour Red Cabbage • Potato Dumplings • Peach Kuchen 79

Chicken with Peach Stuffing • Mustard Salad Dressing • Squash Rings with Green Beans • Orange Meringue Pie...................................81

Autumn Vegetable Beef Stew

This recipe was given to me by a dear friend many years ago. Served with homemade bread and a green salad, it makes a wonderful meal. Even people who don't like turnips find they enjoy their distinctive flavor in this stew.
—Martha Tonnies, Ft. Michell, Kentucky

        1 teaspoon salt
    1/4 teaspoon pepper
    1/4 teaspoon paprika
        1 pound round steak, cut into 1-inch cubes
        1 tablespoon vegetable oil
        1 tablespoon all-purpose flour
1-1/2 cups water
        1 medium onion, chopped
    1/2 cup tomato sauce
        2 beef bouillon cubes
    1/2 teaspoon caraway seeds
        1 bay leaf
        2 medium potatoes, peeled and cut into
           1-inch cubes
        2 medium turnips, peeled and cut into
           1-inch cubes
        2 medium carrots, cut into 1-inch slices

Combine salt, pepper and paprika; toss with beef. In a large saucepan over medium heat, brown beef in oil. Sprinkle with flour; stir well. Add water, onion, tomato sauce, bouillon, caraway seeds and bay leaf. Cover and simmer for 1 hour.

Add potatoes, turnips and carrots; cover and simmer 45 minutes longer or until meat and vegetables are tender. Discard bay leaf. **Yield:** 4-6 servings.

Lemony Marinated Vegetables

Making this salad was a good way to ensure that my daughters and other picky eaters would eat—and enjoy—their vegetables. I prepare it for picnics, simple buffets and the holidays. It's so colorful and tasty.
—Helen Vail, Glenside, Pennsylvania

        1 cup fresh brussels sprouts
    1/2 pound carrots, cut into 1/2-inch slices
        3 cups cauliflowerets
1-1/2 cups broccoli florets
        3 tablespoons lemon juice
        2 teaspoons vegetable oil
        2 teaspoons minced fresh parsley
        1 garlic clove, minced
        1 lemon peel strip, 2-1/2 inches x 1/2 inch
    1/2 teaspoon dried oregano
    1/2 teaspoon dried basil
    1/2 teaspoon salt
    1/8 teaspoon pepper
        2 cups cherry tomatoes

Place brussels sprouts and carrots in a large saucepan; add 1 in. of water. Bring to a boil; cook for 3 minutes. Add cauliflower and broccoli; return to a boil. Cook for 5 minutes or until vegetables are crisp-tender. Rinse in cold water; drain.

In a large bowl, combine lemon juice, oil, parsley, garlic, lemon peel, oregano, basil, salt and pepper. Add cooked vegetables and the tomatoes; toss to coat. Cover and refrigerate for at least 8 hours. Discard lemon peel. **Yield:** 6-8 servings.

Crusty Rolls

I told my sister-in-law I missed the crispy rolls I used to buy from the baker, so she tracked down the recipe for me!
—Charles Steers, Anaheim, California

        1 package (1/4 ounce) active dry yeast
        1 cup warm water (110° to 115°)
        2 tablespoons shortening
        1 tablespoon sugar
        1 teaspoon salt
3-1/2 to 4 cups all-purpose flour
        2 egg whites
Cornmeal

In a mixing bowl, dissolve yeast in water. Add shortening, sugar, salt and 1 cup flour; beat until smooth. Add egg whites; mix well. Add enough remaining flour to form a soft dough.

Turn onto a floured surface; knead until smooth and elastic, about 6-8 minutes (dough will be stiff). Place in a greased bowl, turning once to grease top. Cover and let rise in a warm place until doubled, about 1-1/2 hours.

Punch dough down; divide into 24 pieces and shape into balls. Sprinkle greased baking sheets with cornmeal. Place rolls 2 in. apart on baking sheets. Cover and let rise until doubled, about 30 minutes. Place a large shallow pan filled with boiling water on lowest rack in oven. Bake rolls on middle rack at 425° for 10-11 minutes or until golden brown. **Yield:** 2 dozen.

Country Plum Crumble

My grandmother shared this recipe with me over 30 years ago. It was one of her favorites, and it always earned her compliments. Now history has repeated itself! I've given this recipe to many friends. —*Shari Dore Brantford, Ontario*

        1 cup canned plums, drained
    1/4 cup all-purpose flour
    1/4 cup sugar
    1/8 teaspoon salt
    1/8 teaspoon ground nutmeg
    1/4 cup cold butter *or* margarine
    1/2 cup crushed cornflakes
Half-and-half cream, optional

Cut the plums in half; discard pits. Divide equally between four well-greased 6-oz. custard cups. In a bowl, combine the flour, sugar, salt and nutmeg; cut in butter until mixture is crumbly. Stir in cornflakes; sprinkle over plums. Bake at 350° for 40 minutes or until the topping is golden brown. Serve warm with cream if desired. **Yield:** 4 servings.

Turkey with Corn-Bread Dressing

The dressing was always my favorite part of my mom's Thanksgiving meal. I can still smell the wonderful aroma that filled the house while the turkey roasted.
—Fae Fisher, Callao, Virginia

        3 cups cornmeal
  4-1/2 teaspoons baking powder
  1-1/2 teaspoons salt
        1 cup self-rising flour*
  1-1/4 cups chopped celery
      1/3 cup chopped onion
      1/2 teaspoon celery seed
        2 cups milk
      1/4 cup shortening, melted
        1 egg
      1/2 cup chopped fresh parsley
        1 to 2 tablespoons poultry seasoning
      3/4 teaspoon pepper
        3 eggs, beaten
        1 cup butter *or* margarine, melted, *divided*
        1 turkey (10 to 12 pounds)

Combine first seven ingredients in a bowl. Combine milk, shortening and egg; add to bowl and mix well. Pour into a greased 13-in. x 9-in. x 2-in. baking pan. Bake at 350° for 50 minutes or until bread tests done. Cool.

Crumble corn bread into a large bowl. Add parsley, poultry seasoning and pepper; toss. Combine beaten eggs and 3/4 cup butter; add to the corn bread mixture, stirring gently to mix.

Just before baking, stuff the turkey with dressing. Skewer or fasten openings. Tie drumsticks together. Place on a rack in a roasting pan. Brush with remaining butter. Place remaining dressing in a greased baking dish; cover and refrigerate until ready to bake.

Bake turkey at 325° for 4-1/2 to 5 hours or until thermometer reads 180°. When turkey begins to brown, cover lightly with a tent of aluminum foil. Bake extra dressing at 325° for 1 hour. Allow turkey to stand for 20 minutes before carving. Remove all dressing to a serving bowl. **Yield:** 8-10 servings (10 cups dressing).

*Editor's Note: As a substitute for 1 cup of self-rising flour, place 1-1/2 teaspoons baking powder and 1/2 teaspoon salt in a measuring cup. Add all-purpose flour to measure 1 cup.

Creamy Broccoli Casserole

Mother called this her secret recipe, and to this day, I'm not quite sure I have all the ingredients she used in it. But it still tastes great. After I was married, this casserole became my husband's favorite vegetable dish.   *—Fae Fisher*

      2 eggs
      1 can (10-3/4 ounces) condensed cream of
        mushroom soup, undiluted
      1 cup mayonnaise
    3/4 cup chopped pecans
      1 medium onion, chopped
      2 packages (10 ounces *each*) frozen chopped
        broccoli, cooked and drained
      1 cup (4 ounces) shredded cheddar cheese
      1 tablespoon butter *or* margarine, melted
    1/4 cup soft bread crumbs

In a bowl, beat eggs; add soup, mayonnaise, pecans and onion. Stir in broccoli; pour into a greased 2-qt. shallow baking dish. Sprinkle with the cheese. Combine butter and bread crumbs; sprinkle on top. Bake, uncovered, at 350° for 30 minutes. **Yield:** 8-10 servings.

Apricot Salad

Colorful gelatin salad adds a spot of brightness to any table. It blends well with this holiday feast.
—Fae Fisher

      2 packages (3 ounces *each*) apricot gelatin
      2 cups boiling water
      1 package (8 ounces) cream cheese, softened
      1 cup milk
      1 can (20 ounces) crushed pineapple,
        undrained
      1 carton (4 ounces) frozen whipped topping,
        thawed

Dissolve gelatin in boiling water and set aside. In a mixing bowl, beat cream cheese until smooth. Gradually beat in milk until smooth. Stir in gelatin. Add pineapple and mix well. Chill. When mixture begins to thicken, fold in whipped topping. Pour into a 2-1/2-qt. serving bowl. Chill for at least 2 hours. **Yield:** 8-10 servings.

Harvest Sweet Potato Pie

Pies were baked a few days before the holiday gathering and then placed in a pie safe on our back porch. My father called this "royal pie", fit for a king with its deliciously different flavor. This is another hand-me-down treasured family recipe.   *—Fae Fisher*

      4 eggs
      1 can (12 ounces) evaporated milk
  1-1/4 cups sugar
    3/4 cup butter *or* margarine, melted
      2 teaspoons ground cinnamon
      2 teaspoons pumpkin pie spice
      1 teaspoon vanilla extract
      1 teaspoon lemon extract
    1/2 teaspoon ground nutmeg
    1/2 teaspoon salt
      4 cups mashed cooked sweet potatoes
      2 unbaked pastry shells (9 inches)
Whipped cream, optional

In a mixing bowl, combine first 10 ingredients; mix well. Beat in sweet potatoes. Pour into pie shells. Bake at 425° for 15 minutes. Reduce heat to 350°; bake 30-35 minutes longer or until a knife inserted near the center comes out clean. Cool completely. Serve with whipped cream if desired. Store in the refrigerator. **Yield:** 12-16 servings.

Herbed Pork Roast

This favorite recipe was one of my dear mother's, and each time I serve it, I'm filled with warm memories. This was our family's celebration roast. Mother served it on birthdays and holidays. The combination of herbs enhances the drippings as well, so I use it to make a flavorful gravy.   —Ruth Bethurum, Ozan, Arkansas

    1 boneless pork loin roast (3-1/2 to 4 pounds)
1/2 teaspoon salt
1/2 teaspoon pepper
1/2 cup water
1/2 cup chicken broth
1/4 cup ketchup
    1 garlic clove, minced
1/4 teaspoon ground mustard
1/4 teaspoon *each* dried marjoram, thyme and rosemary, crushed
    2 large onions, sliced
    1 bay leaf
    1 can (8-3/4 ounces) mushroom stems and pieces, undrained

In a Dutch oven coated with nonstick cooking spray, brown roast over medium heat. Sprinkle with salt and pepper. Combine water, broth, ketchup, garlic and seasonings; pour over roast. Add onions and bay leaf.

Cover and simmer over medium heat for 1-1/2 hours or until a meat thermometer reads 160°. Add mushrooms; heat through. Discard bay leaf. Let stand 10 minutes before slicing. Serve with onions and mushrooms. Thicken pan drippings for gravy if desired. **Yield:** 8-10 servings.

Onion Pie

During my teen years, I lived on my aunt's farm in Illinois. This was one of her delicious dishes, and one of many I enjoyed. I'm so happy I got the recipe and later made it my own family's favorite. It's a wonderful side dish to complement any meat entree.
           —Phyllis Jean Sheeley, Altoona, Illinois

    3 large onions, sliced
    1 tablespoon butter *or* margarine
    3 eggs
    2 cups half-and-half cream
Salt and pepper to taste
Pastry for double-crust pie (9 inches)
    4 bacon strips, cooked and crumbled
1/2 cup shredded cheddar cheese

In a skillet, saute onions in butter until golden brown. In a bowl, beat eggs and cream. Add the onions, salt and pepper.

Line a deep-dish 9-in. pie plate with bottom pastry. Add egg mixture; sprinkle with bacon and cheese. Roll out remaining pastry to fit top of pie; place over filling. Seal and flute the edges; cut slits in top.

Bake at 350° for 55-60 minutes or until crust is golden brown. Let stand 15 minutes before cutting. Refrigerate leftovers. **Yield:** 6-8 servings.

Spinach Pecan Bake

I discovered this recipe while I was on a hunt for a different kind of vegetable dish to serve alongside a variety of entrees. I tried it and declared it a winner. The guests I first served this to also raved, so it has a permanent spot in my recipe file. I've passed on the recipe to a number of people over the years, too.
           —Dorothy Pritchett, Wills Point, Texas

    1 medium onion, finely chopped
1/4 cup butter *or* margarine
    3 packages (10 ounces *each*) frozen leaf spinach, thawed and drained
1/2 cup half-and-half cream
1/2 cup coarsely chopped pecans
1/3 cup dry bread crumbs
    1 teaspoon salt
1/2 teaspoon ground nutmeg
1/8 teaspoon pepper
TOPPING:
1/4 cup dry bread crumbs
    2 tablespoons butter *or* margarine, melted

In a skillet, saute onion in butter until tender. In a large bowl, combine onion, spinach, cream, pecans, bread crumbs, salt, nutmeg and pepper; mix well. Transfer to a greased 1-1/2-qt. baking dish.

In a small bowl, combine the topping ingredients and sprinkle over the spinach mixture. Bake, uncovered, at 350° for 30 minutes or until lightly browned. **Yield:** 6-8 servings.

Chewy Ginger Drop Cookies

This flavorful cookie recipe originated with my grandmother. My mom, an excellent baker, also made these cookies. Then I baked them for my own family...my daughters made them...and now my granddaughters are making them—a true family legacy I'm happy to share with others.
           —Lois Furcron
           Coudersport, Pennsylvania

1/2 cup shortening
1/2 cup sugar
    2 cups all-purpose flour
1/2 teaspoon baking soda
1/2 teaspoon ground ginger
1/4 teaspoon salt
1/2 cup molasses
1/4 cup water
Additional sugar

In a mixing bowl, cream the shortening and sugar. In another bowl, combine the flour, baking soda, ginger and salt. Combine the molasses and water. Add dry ingredients to the creamed mixture alternately with the molasses mixture.

Drop dough by rounded teaspoonfuls 2 in. apart onto greased baking sheets. Sprinkle with sugar. Bake at 350° for 13-15 minutes or until edges are set. Remove to wire racks to cool completely. **Yield:** about 2-1/2 dozen.

Sicilian Meat Roll

My sister-in-law shared this recipe years ago and it became our family's favorite meat loaf. The addition of ham and mozzarella is a colorful surprise and adds terrific flavor. This is always a big hit with company, and the leftovers are good either hot or cold.
—*Mrs. W.G. Dougherty, Crawfordsville, Indiana*

2 eggs
1/2 cup tomato juice
3/4 teaspoon dried oregano
2 garlic cloves, minced
1/4 teaspoon salt
1/4 teaspoon pepper
2 pounds ground beef
3/4 cup soft bread crumbs
2 tablespoons minced fresh parsley
8 thin slices fully cooked ham
1-1/2 cups (6 ounces) shredded mozzarella cheese
3 thin slices mozzarella cheese

In a large bowl, combine eggs, tomato juice, oregano, garlic, salt and pepper. Add beef, bread crumbs and parsley; mix well.

On a piece of heavy-duty foil, pat meat mixture into a 12-in. x 10-in. rectangle. Place the ham and shredded cheese on loaf to within 1/2 in. of edges. Roll up, jelly-roll style, beginning with the short end and peeling foil away while rolling. Place on a greased baking pan with seam side down; seal ends.

Bake, uncovered, at 350° for 1 hour and 10 minutes. Top with sliced cheese; bake 5 minutes longer or until cheese is melted. **Yield:** 8 servings.

Parmesan Noodles

My mother served noodles with cottage cheese as a main dish on many a meatless Friday. I altered the recipe a little as a side dish, but it still makes a good main dish. I especially like to serve it with Swiss steak…the special blend of flavors makes it companionable to any meal, though.
—*Elizabeth Ewan, Parma, Ohio*

2 packages (3 ounces *each*) cream cheese, softened
1/2 cup butter *or* margarine, softened, *divided*
2 tablespoons minced fresh parsley
1 teaspoon dried basil
1/2 teaspoon lemon-pepper seasoning
2/3 cup boiling water
1 garlic clove, minced
6 cups hot cooked thin noodles
2/3 cup grated Parmesan cheese, *divided*
Additional parsley, optional

In a small bowl, combine cream cheese, 2 tablespoons butter, parsley, basil and lemon pepper. Stir in water; keep warm.

In a saucepan, saute garlic in remaining butter until lightly browned. Place noodles in a serving bowl; top with garlic mixture. Sprinkle with half of the Parmesan cheese; toss lightly. Spoon cream sauce over noodles and sprinkle with remaining Parmesan. Garnish with parsley if desired. **Yield:** 8 servings.

Three-Step Salad

If you don't try this refreshing salad, you have missed the best! The crisp greens and bright oranges make it colorful, and the sweet caramelized almonds create a unique crunch. This salad is a special treat for family and company.
—*Les Cunningham*
San Diego, California

1/2 cup sliced almonds
3 tablespoons sugar
6 cups torn romaine
1 can (11 ounces) mandarin oranges, drained
1 cup sliced celery
3 green onions, sliced
DRESSING:
1/2 cup vegetable oil
1/4 cup vinegar
2 to 3 tablespoons sugar
1/2 teaspoon salt
1/2 teaspoon ground mustard
1/4 teaspoon garlic powder

In a small saucepan over medium heat, cook and stir almonds and sugar until almonds are coated and lightly browned, about 4 minutes. Spread the almonds on heavy-duty foil to cool; gently break apart.

In a large salad bowl, combine romaine, oranges, celery and onions. Top with almonds. In a jar with tight-fitting lid, combine dressing ingredients; shake well. Pour over salad and toss gently. **Yield:** 8 servings.

Pull-Apart Herb Bread

The ingredients for this recipe are so simple and the results so spectacular, I'm always willing to share the secret. It's actually a variation of a doughnut recipe I made years ago, using refrigerated biscuits. The best part of having this bread is tearing it apart and eating it warm.
—*Evelyn Kenney, Hamilton, New Jersey*

1 garlic clove, minced
1/4 cup butter *or* margarine, melted
2 tubes (10 to 12 ounces *each*) refrigerated biscuits
1 cup (4 ounces) shredded cheddar cheese
1/4 teaspoon dried basil
1/4 teaspoon fennel seed
1/4 teaspoon dried oregano

In a skillet, saute garlic in butter; set aside. Separate biscuits; place half in an even layer in a greased 9-in. springform pan. Brush with butter mixture; sprinkle with half of the cheese and herbs. Repeat. Place the pan on a baking sheet. Bake at 375° for 20-25 minutes or until golden brown. Remove from the pan; serve warm. **Yield:** 8 servings.

Oven Chicken Stew

I grew up with this entree. It couldn't be easier to prepare, and it turns out delicious every time. It's a hearty fall meal your famiy is sure to enjoy. —Phyllis Sheeley
Altona, Illinois

1 broiler/fryer chicken (3 pounds), cut up
1 cup chicken broth
1 cup water
2 medium carrots, sliced
2 medium onions, chopped
2 celery ribs, sliced
2 teaspoons salt
1/2 teaspoon pepper
1/2 teaspoon dried basil

Place the chicken, broth and water in a Dutch oven or 3-qt. baking dish. Top with carrots, onions and celery; sprinkle with salt, pepper and basil. Cover and bake at 350° for 1-1/2 to 2 hours or until chicken juices run clear. **Yield:** 6 servings.

Sweet Potato Casserole

This is my favorite sweet potato recipe. I got it years ago and revised it to include cinnamon and cardamom. It's a nice change from the usual marshmallow-topped recipes. —Verona Wilder, Marble Hill, Missouri

1-1/2 pounds sweet potatoes, peeled and
quartered
1/2 cup sugar
1/4 cup butter *or* margarine, melted
1/2 cup sweetened condensed milk
3 eggs, lightly beaten
1/2 teaspoon ground cinnamon
1/4 to 1/2 teaspoon ground cardamom
Dash lemon juice

Place the sweet potatoes in a large saucepan or Dutch oven; cover with water. Bring to a boil; cook for 20-25 minutes or until tender. Drain; cool slightly and mash.

Add the sugar, butter, milk, eggs, cinnamon, cardamom and lemon juice. Transfer to a greased 1-1/2-qt. baking dish. Cover and bake at 350° for 45-50 minutes or until set. **Yield:** 4-6 servings.

Green Beans with Zucchini

This tasty combination appears on my table often, especially when zucchini is so abundant.
—Gladys DeBoer, Castleford, Idaho

4 cups cut green beans (1-inch pieces)
1 small onion, diced
1/4 cup butter *or* margarine
2 small zucchini, cut into 1/4-inch slices
4 bacon strips, cooked and crumbled
Salt and pepper to taste

Place beans in a saucepan and cover with water. Bring to a boil; cook, uncovered, for 8-10 minutes or until crisp-tender; drain. In a large skillet, saute onion in butter for 3 minutes. Add the zucchini; cook for 4 minutes. Stir in the bacon, beans, salt and pepper; heat through. **Yield:** 6 servings.

Pumpkin Bread Ring

I've been making this moist bread for years. It looks pretty on the table and provides a nice taste of pumpkin on your menu when you're not planning on pumpkin pie for dessert.
—Theresa Stewart
New Oxford, Pennsylvania

1/4 cup butter (no substitutes), softened
1 cup sugar
1 cup packed brown sugar
4 eggs
1 can (15 ounces) solid-pack pumpkin
3 cups biscuit/baking mix
2 teaspoons ground cinnamon
1/2 teaspoon ground ginger
1/4 teaspoon ground cloves
1/4 teaspoon ground nutmeg
1/4 cup milk
GLAZE:
1/3 cup butter
2 cups confectioners' sugar
1-1/2 teaspoons vanilla extract
4 to 6 tablespoons water

In a mixing bowl, cream butter and sugars. Add the eggs, one at a time, beating well after each addition. Add pumpkin; mix well. Combine the biscuit mix, cinnamon, ginger, cloves and nutmeg; add to the creamed mixture alternately with milk. Pour into a greased 10-in. fluted tube pan.

Bake at 350° for 55-60 minutes or until a toothpick inserted near the center comes out clean. Cool for 10 minutes before removing from pan to wire rack.

For glaze, in a saucepan, cook and stir butter over medium heat for 6-7 minutes or until golden brown. Pour into a mixing bowl; beat in the confectioners' sugar, vanilla extract and enough water to achieve drizzling consistency. Drizzle over the top of the cooled bread. **Yield:** 12-16 servings.

Sweet Potato Savvy

Choose firm sweet potatoes that are small- to medium-sized with smooth, unblemished skins. Large sweet potatoes are often very fibrous. If you use an electric mixer to beat cooked sweet potatoes, the stringy fibers will wind around the beaters, thereby leaving the potatoes smooth.

Barbecued Round Steak

This recipe came from a 1950s television program called Kay's Kitchen. I gave it a try, and my family gave it rave reviews. It makes a colorful entree served with fresh green beans...or try French fries—the sauce is great for dipping! —Ray Sholes, Butler, Pennsylvania

     3 tablespoons all-purpose flour
     1/2 teaspoon salt
     1/2 teaspoon pepper
 1-1/2 pounds round steak, cut into four pieces
     4 teaspoons vegetable oil
     1/2 cup chopped celery
     1/2 cup chopped onion
     1 garlic clove, minced
     1 can (10-3/4 ounces) condensed tomato
        soup, undiluted
     3 tablespoons brown sugar
     2 tablespoons Worcestershire sauce
     1 tablespoon vinegar
     2 teaspoons prepared mustard

In a shallow bowl, combine the flour, salt and pepper; dredge the meat. In a large skillet, brown meat on both sides in oil. Remove and keep warm.

In pan drippings, saute celery, onion and garlic for 3-4 minutes. Combine soup, brown sugar, Worcestershire sauce, vinegar and mustard; stir into vegetables. Return meat to pan. Cover and simmer for 1-1/2 to 2 hours or until meat is tender. **Yield:** 4 servings.

Baked Calico Rice

I found this pretty rice dish in a salad oil ad in the Ladies' Home Journal back in 1948. It's a favorite not only for its good taste, but for its simplicity of preparation. —Dorothy Lama, Lindsay, California

     1 can (28 ounces) diced tomatoes, undrained
     1 cup chopped onion
     1 cup chopped celery
     3/4 cup chopped green pepper
     2/3 cup uncooked long grain rice
     1/3 cup vegetable oil
     1 bay leaf
     1 to 2 teaspoons salt
     1/4 teaspoon pepper

In a 2-qt. baking dish, combine all ingredients; mix well. Cover and bake at 350° for 1 to 1-1/4 hours or until rice is tender, stirring occasionally. Discard bay leaf before serving. **Yield:** 4-6 servings.

Favorite Cabbage Salad

I've been sharing this recipe for over 45 years! It's easy to make, keeps well and is great to take along for potluck suppers. Our family and friends enjoy this cabbage salad whenever I serve it. —Edna Culbertson Jenison, Michigan

     1 small head cabbage, shredded
     1/2 cup chopped green pepper
     1/2 cup chopped onion
     3 tablespoons mayonnaise
     2 tablespoons vinegar
     1 tablespoon sugar
     1/4 teaspoon salt
     4 bacon strips, cooked crumbled

In a large bowl, combine cabbage, green pepper and onion. In a small bowl, combine mayonnaise, vinegar, sugar and salt. Pour over cabbage mixture and toss to coat. Cover and refrigerate for at least 4 hours. Stir in bacon just before serving. **Yield:** 6-8 servings.

Apple Walnut Squares

I make "apple everything" in fall when the new crop is in, and I was happy to add this delicious recipe to my apple dishes. A lady at church shared it with me. Sometimes I'll top the squares with a cream cheese frosting, especially if I'm having company. —Leona Pecoraro Ravenden, Arkansas

     1/2 cup shortening
     1 cup sugar
     1 egg
 1-1/2 cups all-purpose flour
 1-1/2 teaspoons baking soda
     1/2 teaspoon salt
 2-1/2 cups finely chopped peeled tart apples
     1/2 cup packed brown sugar
     1 cup chopped walnuts
     1 teaspoon ground cinnamon
     1 teaspoon vanilla extract

In a mixing bowl, cream shortening and sugar; beat in egg. Combine flour, baking soda and salt; gradually add to the creamed mixture and mix well (dough will be stiff). Stir in apples.

Spread batter into a greased 13-in. x 9-in. x 2-in. baking pan. Combine brown sugar, walnuts, cinnamon and vanilla; sprinkle over batter. Bake at 350° for 30-35 minutes or until golden brown. Cool. Cut into squares. **Yield:** 12-16 servings.

About Apples

Buy firm, well-colored apples with a fresh fragrance. The skins should be tight, smooth and free of bruises and punctures.

Choose the variety by how it'll be used. For example, firmer varieties particularly good for baking are Cortland, Northern Spy, Rome Beauty, Winesap and York Imperial.

Salmon Cakes

Since pinto beans and mashed potatoes were our usual daily fare, salmon was a special treat on Sundays when I was growing up. We ate these cakes fast as Mama could fry them—she couldn't get them off the griddle fast enough. —Imogene Hutton, Norton, Texas

>   2 eggs
> 1/4 cup heavy whipping cream
> 1/4 cup cornmeal
>   2 tablespoons sliced green onions
>   2 tablespoons all-purpose flour
> 1/4 teaspoon baking powder
> Pinch pepper
> 1/2 teaspoon salt, optional
>   1 can (14-3/4 ounces) salmon, drained, skinned and boned
>   1 to 2 tablespoons butter *or* margarine

In a medium bowl, beat the eggs. Add cream, cornmeal, green onions, flour, baking powder, pepper and salt if desired. Flake salmon into bowl; blend gently.

Melt butter in a skillet or griddle; drop salmon mixture by 1/3 cupfuls and fry over medium heat for 5 minutes per side or until lightly browned. Serve hot. **Yield:** 3-4 servings (six patties).

Stovetop Macaroni and Cheese

Mama used Texas Longhorn cheese in this recipe. When the cheese melted, it covered all the macaroni. I loved to dig in and see how many strings of cheese would follow my spoonful. —Imogene Hutton

>   1 package (7 ounces) elbow macaroni
> 1/4 cup butter *or* margarine
> 1/4 cup all-purpose flour
> 1/2 teaspoon salt
> Pinch pepper
>   2 cups milk
>   2 cups (8 ounces) shredded cheddar cheese
> Paprika, optional

Cook macaroni according to package directions. Meanwhile, in a medium saucepan, melt butter over medium heat. Stir in flour, salt and pepper; cook until bubbly.

Gradually add milk; cook and stir until thickened. Stir in cheese until melted. Drain macaroni; add to cheese sauce and stir to coat. Sprinkle with paprika if desired. **Yield:** 4-6 servings.

Creamed Peas

I can still taste these wonderful peas in Mama's delicious white sauce. Our food was pretty plain during the week, so I thought this white sauce made the peas extra fancy and fitting for a Sunday meal. —Imogene Hutton

>   1 tablespoon butter *or* margarine
>   1 tablespoon all-purpose flour

> 1/4 teaspoon salt
> 1/8 teaspoon pepper
> 1/2 cup milk
>   1 teaspoon sugar
>   1 package (10 ounces) frozen peas

In a medium saucepan, melt the butter. Add flour, salt and pepper; cook over low heat until bubbly. Gradually add milk and sugar; cook and stir until thickened.

Cook the peas according to the package directions; drain. Stir into the sauce and heat through. **Yield:** 3-4 servings.

Cornmeal Pie

If Mama had time, she'd make these pies on Saturday night. She always made two so we could have one for dessert on Monday, too. One pie served our family very nicely, and there was never any left over. —Imogene Hutton

>   1 cup butter (no substitutes), softened
> 1-1/2 cups sugar
>   3 eggs
> 1-1/2 cups light corn syrup
> 1/2 cup milk
>   1 teaspoon vanilla extract
> 1/2 cup cornmeal
>   3 tablespoons all-purpose flour
>   2 unbaked pastry shells (9 inches)
> Whipped cream, optional

In a large mixing bowl, cream the butter and sugar. Beat in eggs one at a time. Add corn syrup, milk and vanilla; mix well. Fold in cornmeal and flour. Pour into pastry shells.

Bake at 350° for 25 minutes. Reduce heat to 300°; bake 20-25 minutes longer or until pies test done. Cool. Garnish with whipped cream if desired. **Yield:** 12-16 servings.

Purchasing Pasta

Whether buying fresh or dried pasta, buy only brands made with durum wheat (also called semolina). This is the pasta of preference because it absorbs less water, has a mellow flavor and retains a pleasant "bite" when cooked.

When buying dried pasta, always check the package to make sure the pieces are unbroken. If it looks crumbly or dusty, air has gotten to it and it's stale.

Dried pasta will last almost indefinitely if stored in an airtight glass or plastic container in a cool, dark place.

Cider-Roasted Chicken

I've never shared this recipe before, even with members of my own family. I use it only for special occasions. I found the recipe in the first real good cookbook I owned, and my six children love it. —Mary Dunphy
Stephenville, Newfoundland

1 whole roasting chicken (5 to 7 pounds)
1/4 cup butter *or* margarine
2-1/2 cups apple cider
6 to 8 small unpeeled red potatoes, quartered
6 to 8 small onions, peeled and quartered
1 to 2 medium green peppers, cut into strips
6 to 8 bacon strips
2 to 4 small tomatoes, quartered

Place chicken in a roasting pan; dot with butter. Bake, uncovered, at 375° for 15 minutes. Reduce heat to 325°; bake for 2 hours.

Pour cider over chicken. Add potatoes, onions and peppers to the pan; place bacon over chicken breast. Bake 1 hour longer, basting often.

Add tomatoes to the pan. Bake 30 minutes longer or until a meat thermometer reads 180°. Cover and let stand 10 minutes before carving. Thicken the pan juices for gravy if desired. **Yield:** 6 servings.

Cinnamon Apple Salad

This recipe came from my mother. It's very pretty when cut into squares and served on a lettuce-lined plate. I also like that I can fix it a day ahead of time, especially when preparing a big holiday meal. —Lisa Andis
Morristown, Indiana

1/2 cup red-hot candies
1 cup boiling water
1 package (3 ounces) lemon gelatin
1 cup applesauce
1 package (8 ounces) cream cheese, softened
1/2 cup mayonnaise *or* salad dressing
1/2 cup chopped pecans
1/4 cup chopped celery

In a bowl, dissolve candies in water (reheat if necessary). Add gelatin; stir to dissolve. Stir in applesauce. Pour half into an 8-in. square pan that has been lightly coated with nonstick cooking spray. Refrigerate until firm. Cover and set remaining gelatin mixture aside at room temperature.

Meanwhile, combine the cream cheese, mayonnaise, pecans and celery; spread over chilled gelatin mixture. Carefully pour remaining gelatin mixture over cream cheese layer. Chill overnight. **Yield:** 9 servings.

Butternut Squash Bisque

I'm always improvising on recipes. For this one, I started with a basic creamed vegetable soup, and then added roasted squash and leeks for a distinctive taste. —Dianna Wacasey, Houston, Texas

1 medium butternut squash, peeled, seeded and cut into 1-inch cubes (about 4 cups), *divided*
1/2 cup orange juice
1/3 cup packed brown sugar
1 cinnamon stick (3 inches)
1 cup sliced leeks (white portion only)
1 medium tart apple, peeled and chopped
1/2 cup chopped onion
1/4 cup butter *or* margarine
4 cups chicken broth
1/3 cup heavy whipping cream
Salt and pepper to taste
1 tablespoon olive *or* vegetable oil

In a roasting pan, toss 3 cups of squash, orange juice and brown sugar; add cinnamon. Cover and bake at 450° for 30-40 minutes or until squash is tender. Discard cinnamon; drain squash, reserving cooking liquid. Set squash and liquid aside.

In a Dutch oven, saute leeks, apple and onion in butter until tender. Add broth; bring to a boil. Stir in cooked squash; cook for 5 minutes. Add cream, salt and pepper; heat through. Cool slightly.

In a blender or food processor, process soup in batches until smooth. Return all to the pan; heat through (do not boil). Cut remaining squash into 1/4-in. cubes. In a skillet, saute squash cubes in oil and reserved cooking liquid until squash is tender and liquid has evaporated. Ladle soup into bowls. Garnish with squash cubes. **Yield:** 6 servings.

Pumpkin Custard

This dessert is a refreshing departure from pumpkin pie, but it has the same good old-fashioned flavor. It's a cinch to prepare even on your busiest days and especially good after a hearty holiday meal.
—Andrea Holcomb, Torrington, Connecticut

1 can (15 ounces) solid-pack pumpkin
2 eggs
1 cup half-and-half cream
2/3 cup packed brown sugar
1-1/2 teaspoons pumpkin pie spice
1/2 teaspoon salt
TOPPING:
1/4 cup packed brown sugar
1/4 cup chopped pecans
1 tablespoon butter *or* margarine, melted
Whipped cream and ground cinnamon, optional

In a mixing bowl, combine the first six ingredients; beat until smooth. Pour into four greased 10-oz. custard cups. Place in a 13-in. x 9-in. x 2-in. baking pan; pour hot water around cups to a depth of 1 in. Bake, uncovered, at 350° for 20 minutes.

Meanwhile, in a small bowl, combine the brown sugar, pecans and butter. Sprinkle over custard. Bake 30-35 minutes longer or until a knife inserted near the center comes out clean. Serve warm or chilled; top with whipped cream and cinnamon if desired. **Yield:** 4 servings.

Spiced Pot Roast

I always looked forward to Sunday dinner at my grand-parents' house, because Grandmother was the best cook anywhere. All her meals were delicious, but I especially loved dinners featuring this savory pot roast.
—Frances Wilson, Tulsa, Oklahoma

    1/3 cup all-purpose flour
      1 teaspoon salt
    1/4 teaspoon pepper
      1 boneless beef rump *or* chuck roast
        (3 pounds)
      2 tablespoons vegetable oil
  1-1/2 cups beef broth
    1/2 cup chutney
    1/2 cup raisins
    1/2 cup chopped onion
  1-1/2 teaspoons curry powder
    1/2 teaspoon garlic powder
    1/2 teaspoon ground ginger

Combine flour, salt and pepper; rub over entire roast. In a Dutch oven, brown roast in oil on all sides. Combine remaining ingredients and pour over roast. Cover and bake at 325° for 3 hours or until meat is tender. Thicken gravy if desired. **Yield:** 6-8 servings.

Grandma's Apples and Rice

Like most women of her generation, my husband's grandmother was a "no-measure cook". This recipe of hers suffered as it was handed down, so I tried to work out the kinks. My husband pronounced the results as good as he remembered, and we declared it the "official" recipe. *—Joan Kasura, Silver Spring, Maryland*

  1-1/4 cups uncooked brown rice
      4 tablespoons butter *or* margarine, *divided*
  2-1/2 cups chunky applesauce
      1 cup cubed peeled apples
    1/4 cup packed brown sugar
  1-3/4 teaspoons ground cinnamon, *divided*
Dash salt

Cook rice according to package directions. Stir 2 tablespoons butter into hot rice. Add applesauce, apples, brown sugar, 1-1/2 teaspoons cinnamon and salt.

Spoon into a greased 2-qt. baking dish. Dot with remaining butter; sprinkle with remaining cinnamon. Bake, uncovered, at 350° for 35 minutes or until heated through. Serve warm or cold. **Yield:** 6-8 servings.

Turnip Souffle

Although my grandmother lived in the city, she always tended a large vegetable garden. Toward the end of summer, we helped her pick the vegetables for our favorite dishes. Like most kids, we didn't care much for turnips, but when Grandmother fixed them this way, we'd ask for seconds. *—Dorothy Dick, St. Louis, Missouri*

  1-1/2 pounds turnips (about 6 medium), peeled
        and sliced
  1-1/2 teaspoons salt, *divided*
    1/2 teaspoon sugar
    1/2 cup butter *or* margarine
      2 tablespoons all-purpose flour
    2/3 cup milk
      4 eggs, *separated*
      3 bacon strips, cooked and crumbled

Place the turnips, 1/2 teaspoon of salt and sugar in a saucepan; cover with water. Cover and cook until the turnips are tender, about 15-20 minutes; drain well and mash (do not add milk or butter). Set aside.

In another saucepan, melt butter; stir in the flour and remaining salt until smooth. Add milk; bring to a boil. Cook and stir for 2 minutes. Beat egg yolks in a small bowl; gradually stir in 1/2 cup hot milk mixture. Return all to pan; cook and stir for 1 minute. Stir in turnips; remove from the heat. Beat egg whites until stiff peaks form; fold into batter.

Spoon into a greased 11-in. x 7-in. x 2-in. baking dish. Sprinkle with bacon. Bake, uncovered, at 350° for 30 minutes or until souffle is golden brown. **Yield:** 6-8 servings.

Baking Powder Biscuits

When I was growing up, Mother made these wonderful biscuits often. Some time ago, I consulted her box of old recipes and was delighted to find this childhood favorite. *—Catherine Yoder, Bertha, Minnesota*

      2 cups all-purpose flour
      2 tablespoons sugar
      4 teaspoons baking powder
    1/2 teaspoon cream of tartar
    1/2 teaspoon salt
    1/2 cup shortening
      1 egg
    2/3 cup milk

In a large bowl, combine flour, sugar, baking powder, cream of tartar and salt. Cut in the shortening until mixture resembles coarse crumbs. Beat egg and milk; stir into dry ingredients just until moistened.

Turn onto a lightly floured surface; roll to 1/2-in. thickness. Cut with a 2-1/2-in. biscuit cutter; place on an ungreased baking sheet. Bake at 450° for 10-12 minutes or until golden brown. **Yield:** 10 biscuits.

Turnip Tips

Before using, trim turnip stem and root ends. Turnips should be peeled and cut up before cooking.

Stuffed Turkey Roll

When a friend gave me some ground turkey to use up, I looked for an inventive way to prepare it. I found this recipe while scouring through my collection.
—Patricia Eckard, Singers Glen, Virginia

    1 egg, lightly beaten
1/2 cup quick-cooking oats
1/2 teaspoon salt
1/8 teaspoon pepper
    1 pound ground turkey
1/4 cup chopped onion
1/4 cup chopped celery
    3 tablespoons butter *or* margarine
    2 tablespoons water
1/2 teaspoon rubbed sage
1/4 teaspoon ground thyme
    2 cups seasoned stuffing cubes
    2 bacon strips, halved

In a bowl, combine the egg, oats, salt and pepper. Crumble turkey over mixture and mix well. Pat into a 12-in. x 9-in. rectangle on a piece of heavy-duty foil; set aside.

In a saucepan, saute onion and celery in butter until tender. Remove from the heat. Stir in water, sage and thyme. Add stuffing; mix well. Spoon over turkey to within 1 in. of edges. Roll up, jelly-roll style, starting with a short side and peeling away foil while rolling.

Place loaf, seam side down, in a greased 9-in. x 5-in. x 3-in. loaf pan. Place bacon strips over top. Bake, uncovered, at 325° for 60-70 minutes or until meat is no longer pink and a meat thermometer reads 165°. **Yield:** 4 servings.

Peppered Green Beans

I like the tangy taste of these green beans. The combination of flavors enhances the beans, and the colors make this side dish an attractive addition to any entree.
—Chet Sioda, Tacoma, Washington

    1 medium sweet red pepper, julienned
    1 medium onion, julienned
    1 tablespoon olive *or* vegetable oil
    1 package (16 ounces) frozen cut green beans
    2 tablespoons cider vinegar
1/8 teaspoon crushed red pepper flakes,
        optional
Salt and pepper to taste

In a skillet, saute red pepper and onion in oil until crisp-tender. Add beans; cook and stir for 10-12 minutes or until heated through. Remove from the heat; drain. Stir in vinegar, pepper flakes if desired, salt and pepper. **Yield:** 6-8 servings.

Louisiana Sweet Potato Casserole

*This recipe is a hand-me-down from my mother. My dad used to plant a lot of sweet potatoes, so Mother be-*came quite creative in preparing them. It's our annual holiday dish with turkey and trimmings, but when I have a taste for something sweet, I reach into my file for this recipe.*
—Aline Fazzio, Houma, Louisiana

    4 eggs, beaten
    1 cup sugar
    1 cup milk
1/4 cup butter *or* margarine, melted
    3 tablespoons all-purpose flour
1/4 teaspoon *each* salt, ground cinnamon,
        nutmeg and allspice
    3 cups shredded uncooked sweet potatoes

In a bowl, combine the eggs, sugar, milk and butter. Combine the flour, salt, cinnamon, nutmeg and allspice; stir into the egg mixture with sweet potatoes. Transfer to a greased 8-in. square baking dish.

Bake, uncovered, at 350° for 40-45 minutes or until a knife inserted near the center comes out clean. **Yield:** 6-8 servings.

Berry Cheesecake Parfaits

I can serve up this easy dessert in no time. Impressive and delicious, it seems to be just the right touch after a full meal. We also recommend it as a great midnight snack.
—Joyce Mart, Wichita, Kansas

    1 package (8 ounces) cream cheese, softened
    2 to 4 tablespoons sugar
1/2 cup vanilla yogurt
    2 cups fresh raspberries *or* berries of your
        choice
1/2 cup graham cracker crumbs (8 squares)

In a mixing bowl, beat cream cheese and sugar until smooth. Stir in yogurt. In parfait glasses or bowls, alternate layers of berries, cream cheese mixture and cracker crumbs. Serve immediately or refrigerate for up to 8 hours. **Yield:** 4 servings.

Talking Turkey

Bacteria on raw poultry can contaminate other food it comes in contact with, so it's vital you always use hot soapy water to thoroughly wash your hands, countertops and any utensils used in the preparation of poultry.

Ground turkey may be substituted for ground beef or combined with ground beef in many recipes. Store it in the coldest part of the refrigerator for 1 to 2 days. Dishes featuring this ground meat should always be cooked to an internal temperature of 165°.

About 45 million turkeys are consumed each Thanksgiving.

Sauerbraten

Each year, Dad, Mom and we kids would help prepare this special meal around the holidays.
—Barbara White, Cross Plains, Wisconsin

    1 tablespoon whole peppercorns
    1 tablespoon whole allspice
    1 tablespoon salt
    1 beef rump roast (4 to 5 pounds)
    4 bacon strips, diced
    1 cup vinegar
    1 cup water
   12 whole peppercorns
   12 whole allspice
    1 large onion, sliced
    2 bay leaves
    1 jar (12 ounces) plum preserves
    2 gingersnaps, crushed
    1 cup beef broth *or* port wine
  1/2 cup all-purpose flour

Place the tablespoon of peppercorns and allspice in a cloth bag; pound to a powder with a hammer. Mix in salt; rub over roast. Set aside.

In a large Dutch oven, cook bacon for 3-4 minutes; push to edge of pan. Add roast; brown on all sides. Add vinegar, water, whole peppercorns and allspice, onion and bay leaves; bring to a boil. Reduce heat; cover and simmer for 2 hours. Stir in preserves and gingersnaps; cook 1 hour longer or until meat is tender. Chill roast overnight in cooking liquid.

The next day, skim off fat. Heat roast slowly in cooking liquid until heated through, about 1 hour. Remove roast and keep warm. Strain cooking liquid; return 3-1/2 cups to pan. Combine broth or wine and flour; stir into cooking liquid. Cook and stir until thickened and bubbly; cook and stir 1 minute more. Slice roast and serve with gravy. **Yield:** 12-14 servings.

Sweet-and-Sour Red Cabbage

I helped Mother shred the cabbage and cut up the apples for this recipe. The touch of tartness is wonderful with the sauerbraten. *—Barbara White*

    2 tablespoons bacon drippings *or*
        vegetable oil
  1/4 cup packed brown sugar
    3 tablespoons vinegar
    1 cup water
  1/4 teaspoon salt
Dash pepper
    4 cups shredded red cabbage
    2 apples, peeled and sliced

In a large skillet, combine drippings or oil, brown sugar, vinegar, water, salt and pepper. Cook for 2-3 minutes or until hot, stirring occasionally. Add cabbage; cover and cook for 10 minutes over medium-low heat, stirring occasionally. Add apples; cook, uncovered, for about 10 minutes more or until tender, stirring occasionally. **Yield:** 6-8 servings.

Potato Dumplings

When I was a child, I loved to watch the cooking dumplings pop to the top of the pot of boiling water.
—Barbara White

CROUTONS:
  1/4 cup butter *or* margarine
    3 slices dry bread, cut into small cubes
DUMPLINGS:
    4 medium potatoes, peeled and quartered
    1 cup all-purpose flour
    1 teaspoon baking powder
    1 teaspoon salt
    2 teaspoons ground nutmeg
    2 eggs, lightly beaten
    2 teaspoons butter *or* margarine
    2 tablespoons dry bread crumbs

For croutons, melt butter in a small skillet; brown bread cubes. Set aside. In a saucepan, boil potatoes in water to cover until tender. Cool; mash potatoes and place in a large bowl. Add flour, baking powder, salt and nutmeg. Stir in eggs; beat until mixture holds its shape.

With lightly floured hands, shape about 2 tablespoons dough into a ball, placing a few croutons in center of each ball. Repeat with remaining dough and croutons. Refrigerate for 1 hour.

Drop dumplings into boiling salted water (2 tablespoons salt to 1 quart water). Simmer, uncovered for 10 minutes. Drain. Melt butter in a small skillet; cook and stir the bread crumbs until lightly browned. Sprinkle over dumplings. **Yield:** 15 dumplings.

Peach Kuchen

Kuchen is a fitting dessert for this German meal. It's not too sweet, and you can use virtually any of your favorite fruits. *—Barbara White*

CRUST:
    1 cup all-purpose flour
  1/4 cup confectioners' sugar
  1/4 teaspoon salt
  1/2 cup butter *or* margarine
FILLING:
    2 cans (one 29 ounces, one 16 ounces) sliced
        peaches, drained
    2 eggs
    1 cup sugar
  1/4 teaspoon salt
    3 tablespoons all-purpose flour
    1 cup (8 ounces) sour cream

In a bowl, combine flour, confectioners' sugar and salt. Cut in butter to form a dough. Pat lightly into an ungreased 11-in. x 7-in. x 2-in. baking pan. Arrange peaches over the crust; set aside. In another bowl, beat eggs. Whisk in sugar, salt, flour and sour cream until mixture is smooth. Pour over the peaches. Bake at 450° for 10 minutes. Reduce heat to 325°; bake 35 minutes more or until center is set. Serve warm or chilled. Store in the refrigerator. **Yield:** 8-10 servings.

Chicken with Peach Stuffing

This is my favorite kind of recipe…something that tastes so good, yet requires a minimum of preparation. This simple dish is just right, now that my husband and I are empty nesters, yet it's elegant enough to serve for company. —Theresa Stewart, New Oxford, Pennsylvania

  1 can (15-1/4 ounces) sliced peaches
  4 boneless skinless chicken breast halves
  2 tablespoons vegetable oil
  2 tablespoons butter *or* margarine
  1 tablespoon brown sugar
  1 tablespoon cider vinegar
  1/8 teaspoon ground allspice
  3 cups instant chicken-flavored stuffing mix

Drain peaches, reserving juice; set the peaches aside. Add enough water to juice to measure 1 cup; set aside.

In a skillet, brown chicken on both sides in oil. Gradually stir in peach juice mixture, butter, brown sugar, vinegar and allspice. Bring to a boil. Reduce heat; cover and simmer 5 minutes or until chicken juices run clear.

Stir in stuffing mix and peaches. Cover and remove from the heat. Let stand for 5 minutes or until liquid is absorbed. **Yield:** 4 servings.

Mustard Salad Dressing

My cousin shared this recipe after I commented on its mild, delicious taste. It's so easy to whisk up, and it stores well in the refrigerator. —Ruth Ann Stelfox Raymond, Alberta

  1/2 cup mayonnaise *or* salad dressing
  2 tablespoons sugar
  1 tablespoon white vinegar
  1-1/2 teaspoons prepared mustard
Salad greens and vegetables of your choice

In a bowl, whisk the mayonnaise, sugar, vinegar and mustard until well blended. Cover and refrigerate until serving. Serve with salad. **Yield:** 1 cup.

Squash Rings with Green Beans

I wanted to make a colorful vegetable for Christmas dinner one year and came up with this combination. It was a big hit with our guests. Even my nephew, who attended culinary school, was impressed! —Joan Sieck, Rensselaer, New York

  2 medium acorn squash (about 2 pounds *each*)
  3/4 teaspoon salt, *divided*
  1/4 teaspoon pepper, *divided*
  1/4 cup plus 2 tablespoons butter *or* margarine, *divided*
  1/2 cup packed brown sugar
  2 tablespoons water
  1 pound fresh green beans, cut into 1-1/2-inch pieces

  1/4 teaspoon dried basil
  1/4 teaspoon dried rosemary, crushed

Cut squash into 1-in. slices; discard seeds and ends. Arrange slices in a single layer in a greased 15-in. x 10-in. x 1-in. baking pan. Sprinkle with 1/4 teaspoon salt and 1/8 teaspoon pepper. Cover and bake at 350° for 40 minutes.

Meanwhile, in a saucepan, combine 1/4 cup butter, brown sugar and water; bring to a boil. Brush over the squash. Bake, uncovered, for 15 minutes or until tender, basting frequently.

Place beans in a saucepan; cover with water. Bring to a boil. Cook 10 minutes or until tender; drain. Add basil, rosemary, and remaining butter, salt and pepper. Spoon into squash rings. **Yield:** 6 servings.

Orange Meringue Pie

I found this recipe while vacationing in Florida. I made a few changes and added lime juice for extra tartness. —June Nehmer, Las Vegas, Nevada

1-1/2 cups graham cracker crumbs (about 24 squares)
  1/4 cup sugar
  1/3 cup butter *or* margarine, melted
FILLING:
  1 cup sugar
  1/4 cup cornstarch
  1/4 teaspoon salt
  1 cup orange juice
  1/2 cup water
  3 egg yolks, well beaten
  2 tablespoons lime juice
  4 teaspoons grated orange peel
  1 tablespoon butter *or* margarine
MERINGUE:
  3 egg whites
  1/8 teaspoon cream of tartar
  6 tablespoons sugar

In a bowl, combine the cracker crumbs and sugar; stir in butter. Press onto the bottom and up the sides of a 9-in. pie plate. Bake at 375° for 8-10 minutes or until lightly browned. Cool.

For filling, combine the sugar, cornstarch and salt in a saucepan. Whisk in orange juice and water until smooth. Cook and stir over medium heat until thickened and bubbly. Reduce heat; cook and stir 2 minutes longer. Remove from the heat. Gradually stir 1 cup hot filling into egg yolks; return all to the pan, stirring constantly. Bring to a gentle boil; cook and stir for 2 minutes. Remove from the heat; stir in the lime juice, orange peel and butter. Pour hot filling into pie crust.

For the meringue, beat egg whites in a mixing bowl until foamy. Add cream of tartar; beat on medium speed until soft peaks form. Gradually beat in sugar, 1 tablespoon at a time, on high until stiff peaks form. Spread over hot filling, sealing edges to crust. Bake at 350° for 12-15 minutes or until golden. Cool on a wire rack for 1 hour; refrigerate for 1-2 hours before serving. Refrigerate leftovers. **Yield:** 6-8 servings.

pp. 94-95

pp. 84-85

pp. 92-93

pp. 104-105

Winter Meals

Slow-Cooked Cherry Pork Chops • Apple Mashed Potatoes • Marjoram Green Beans • Choco-Scotch Marble Cake.........................85

Beef Rouladen • Greens 'n' Grapefruit Salad • Bacon-Topped Brussels Sprouts • Strawberry Schaum Torte......................87

New England Salmon Pie • Ruby-Red Beet Salad • Mushroom Broccoli Medley • Molasses Cutouts 89

Classic Chili • Cheddar Chive Bread • Garden Olive Salad • Easy Cranberry Pie 91

Creamed Turkey Over Rice • Special Scalloped Corn • Fruity Lime Salad Mold • Gingerbread with Brown Sugar Sauce 93

Barbecued Pot Roast • Poppy Seed Cheese Bread • Tomato Crouton Casserole • Sour Cream Drops.......................................95

Turkey Apple Potpie • Wild Rice and Squash Pilaf • Cranberry Relish Salad • Soft Mincemeat Cookies......................................97

Lamb Chops with Prunes • Blue-Ribbon Herb Rolls • Spinach Cheese Bake • Chocolate Yum-Yum Cake 99

Golden Pancakes • Onion Brunch Squares • Saucy Fruit Medley • Danish Coffee Cake 101

Mother's Pasties • Special Creamed Corn • Bacon-Swiss Tossed Salad • Raisin-Filled Torte...103

Baked Ham and Apples • Minty Peas and Onions • Skillet Herb Bread • Holiday Gumdrop Cookies 105

Cranberry Meatballs • Zippy Cheese Dip • Rosy Fruit Punch • Ham Salad Spread.......107

Slow-Cooked Cherry Pork Chops

I mixed and matched several recipes to come up with this one. I'm always happy to adapt recipes for my slow cooker. It's so easy to prepare a meal that way.
—Mildred Sherrer, Bay City, Texas

6 bone-in pork loin chops (3/4 inch thick)
1/8 teaspoon salt
Dash pepper
1 cup canned cherry pie filling
2 teaspoons lemon juice
1/2 teaspoon chicken bouillon granules
1/8 teaspoon ground mace

In a skillet coated with nonstick cooking spray, brown the pork chops over medium heat on both sides. Season with salt and pepper.

In a slow cooker, combine pie filling, lemon juice, bouillon and mace. Add pork chops. Cover and cook on low for 3-4 hours or until meat is no longer pink. **Yield:** 6 servings.

Apple Mashed Potatoes

I love potatoes...especially mashed. When I came up with this combination, it was declared a winner. I serve this as a side dish when I have pork as an entree.
—Rebecca Page, Pensacola, Florida

4 medium potatoes, peeled and cubed
2 medium tart apples, peeled and quartered
1/2 teaspoon salt
4 bacon strips, diced
1 small onion, quartered and thinly sliced
1/4 cup butter *or* margarine
1 teaspoon cider vinegar
1/2 teaspoon sugar
Dash ground nutmeg

Place the potatoes, apples and salt in a large saucepan; add enough water to cover. Bring to a boil; cover and cook for 12 minutes or until tender. Meanwhile, in a small skillet, cook bacon over medium heat until crisp. Remove to paper towels; drain, reserving 1 teaspoon drippings. In the drippings, saute onion until tender.

Drain the potatoes and apples. Add the butter, vinegar and sugar; mash until smooth. Top with onion, bacon and nutmeg. **Yield:** 4-6 servings.

Marjoram Green Beans

This easy-to-do vegetable dish becomes memorable with the addition of marjoram. The taste is subtle, yet distinctive. I like to fix beans this way for special dinners, since the bright green is so pretty on the plate.
—Charlene Griffin, Minocqua, Wisconsin

1-1/2 pounds fresh green beans, cut into 1-inch pieces
3/4 cup water
3 tablespoons butter *or* margarine

1/2 teaspoon salt
1/4 teaspoon pepper
1/8 to 1/4 teaspoon dried marjoram

Place beans and water in a large saucepan; bring to a boil. Reduce heat; cover and cook for 8-10 minutes or until crisp-tender. Drain. Add butter, salt, pepper and marjoram; stir until butter is melted. **Yield:** 6-8 servings.

Choco-Scotch Marble Cake

This recipe was given to me many years ago by a friend. Teaming chocolate with butterscotch for a marble cake makes it more flavorful and colorful than the usual chocolate-vanilla combination. This rich family favorite is very moist and keeps well.
—Pam Giammattei, Valatie, New York

1 package (18-1/4 ounces) yellow cake mix
1 package (3.4 ounces) instant butterscotch pudding mix
4 eggs
1 cup (8 ounces) sour cream
1/3 cup vegetable oil
1/2 cup butterscotch chips
1 square (1 ounce) unsweetened chocolate, melted
FROSTING:
1-1/2 cups butterscotch chips, melted
1 square (1 ounce) unsweetened chocolate, melted
5 to 6 tablespoons half-and-half cream
2 tablespoons finely chopped pecans

In a large mixing bowl, combine cake mix, pudding mix, eggs, sour cream and oil; beat on low speed for 2 minutes. Divide batter in half; stir butterscotch chips into half and chocolate into the other half. Spoon half of the butterscotch batter in a greased 10-in. fluted tube pan; top with half of the chocolate batter. Repeat layers. Cut through batter with a knife to swirl.

Bake at 350° for 40-45 minutes or until a toothpick inserted near the center comes out clean. Cool for 10 minutes before removing from pan to a wire rack to cool completely.

For frosting, combine butterscotch chips and chocolate in a small mixing bowl. Beat in enough cream until the frosting is smooth and reaches desired spreading consistency. Spread over top of cake. Sprinkle with pecans. **Yield:** 12-16 servings.

Cake Clue

If a chocolate cake recipe calls for greasing and flouring the pan, dust it with unsweetened cocoa powder instead of flour.

Beef Rouladen

I have used this recipe for years and rely on it when we have company. It's a dish that can be prepared ahead of time and makes a good hearty meal when cold weather sets in. —Jeanne Davis, Hardin, Montana

        2 cups sliced onions
        4 tablespoons vegetable oil, *divided*
        6 bacon strips
        6 beef round *or* sirloin tip steaks (about 1/4
          pound *each*)
    1/2 teaspoon salt
    1/4 teaspoon pepper
        1 tablespoon Dijon mustard
        6 dill pickle spears
    3/4 cup all-purpose flour
 1-1/3 cups water
        4 teaspoons beef bouillon granules
        1 teaspoon dried thyme
        1 bay leaf
        1 tablespoon butter *or* margarine, melted
Hot cooked noodles

In a large skillet, saute onions in 2 tablespoons of oil until tender; remove with a slotted spoon and set aside. In the same skillet, cook bacon for 3-4 minutes or until partially cooked but not crisp. Remove and set aside.

Pound steaks to 1/4-in. thickness; sprinkle with salt and pepper. Spread with mustard and top with sauteed onions. Place a pickle at one short end and a bacon strip lengthwise on top. Roll up jelly-roll style; secure with toothpicks. Set aside 1 tablespoon flour for thickening. Coat the roll-ups with remaining flour.

In the skillet, heat remaining oil over medium heat; brown roll-ups on all sides. Add water, bouillon, thyme and bay leaf. Bring to a boil. Reduce heat; cover and simmer 30 minutes or until beef is tender.

Remove roll-ups and keep warm. Combine butter and reserved flour; add to the pan juices. Bring to a boil; cook and stir for 2 minutes or until thickened. Discard bay leaf and toothpicks. Serve beef and gravy over noodles. **Yield:** 6 servings.

Greens 'n' Grapefruit Salad

We live in Florida during the winter and can pick fresh grapefruit on our property. This salad is a refreshing side dish. —Patty Kile, Greentown, Pennsylvania

        4 cups torn salad greens
        2 tablespoons chopped red onion
        1 medium grapefruit, peeled and sectioned
    1/2 cup sliced fresh mushrooms
    1/2 cup sliced water chestnuts
DRESSING:
    1/2 cup mayonnaise *or* salad dressing
    1/4 cup Catalina salad dressing
    1/4 cup sesame seeds, toasted
        2 tablespoons sugar
        2 tablespoons cider vinegar

In a salad bowl, combine the greens, onion, grapefruit, mushrooms and water chestnuts. In a small bowl, whisk together the dressing ingredients. Drizzle over salad; serve immediately. **Yield:** 4-6 servings.

Bacon-Topped Brussels Sprouts

I love brussels sprouts and used to grow them in our garden. I created this recipe myself, but I'm always on the lookout for other new ways to prepare sprouts. —Lynne Howard, Annandale, Virginia

        1 package (16 ounces) frozen brussels
          sprouts
        2 tablespoons butter *or* margarine, melted
    1/2 teaspoon garlic salt
    1/4 teaspoon onion powder
    1/4 teaspoon dried oregano
    1/2 pound sliced bacon, cooked and crumbled

Cook brussels sprouts according to package directions; drain. Add butter, garlic salt, onion powder and oregano; toss. Place in a serving dish. Top with bacon. **Yield:** 4-6 servings.

Strawberry Schaum Torte

This recipe was handed down from my German grandma. She took great pride in serving this delicate dessert. Whenever I make it, I'm filled with warm memories of childhood. —Diane Krisman, Hales Corners, Wisconsin

        8 egg whites (about 1 cup)
        2 cups sugar
        1 tablespoon white vinegar
        1 teaspoon vanilla extract
    1/4 teaspoon salt
Sliced fresh strawberries
Whipped cream

In a large mixing bowl, beat egg whites on high speed until soft peaks form. Reduce speed to medium. Add sugar, 2 tablespoons at a time, beating until stiff and glossy peaks form. Beat in vinegar, vanilla and salt.

Spread into a greased 10-in. springform pan. Bake at 300° for 65-70 minutes or until lightly browned. Remove to a wire rack to cool (meringue will fall). Serve with strawberries and whipped cream. Store leftovers in the refrigerator. **Yield:** 10-12 servings.

Editor's Note: This recipe requires a stand mixer.

Beating Egg Whites

It's easiest to separate eggs when they're cold, but egg whites will reach their fullest volume if they stand at room temperature for 30 minutes before beating.

New England Salmon Pie

My mom always made salmon pie on Christmas Eve. Now I bake this dish for the holidays and other get-togethers during the year. It takes little time to prepare, and with a salad on the side, it makes a satisfying meal.
—*Jeanne Uttley, Salem, New Hampshire*

    3-1/2 cups warm mashed potatoes (prepared
            without milk and butter)
        1 medium onion, finely chopped
    1/3 cup milk
    1/2 teaspoon celery seed
    1/2 teaspoon garlic powder
    1/2 teaspoon salt
    1/4 teaspoon white pepper
        1 can (14-3/4 ounces) salmon, drained, bones
            and skin removed
        2 tablespoons minced fresh parsley
Pastry for double-crust pie (9 inches)
        1 egg
        1 tablespoon water

In a bowl, combine the potatoes, onion, milk, celery seed, garlic powder, salt and pepper. Stir in salmon and parsley. Line a 9-in. pie plate with bottom pastry; trim even with edges. Spread salmon mixture into crust.

Roll out remaining pastry to fit top of pie; place over filling. Trim, seal and flute edges. Cut slits in top. Beat egg and water; brush over pastry. Bake at 350° for 40-45 minutes or until crust is golden. Refrigerate leftovers. **Yield:** 6-8 servings.

Ruby-Red Beet Salad

Adapted from a recipe that I've had for about 30 years, this salad was a big hit when I served it to my future in-laws. —*Toni Talbott, Fairbanks, Alaska*

        1 package (3 ounces) cherry gelatin
        1 package (3 ounces) raspberry gelatin
        1 package (3 ounces) strawberry gelatin
        4 cups boiling water
        1 can (20 ounces) crushed pineapple
        1 can (15 ounces) diced beets, drained
DRESSING:
    1/2 cup mayonnaise
    1/2 cup sour cream
        3 tablespoons *each* chopped celery, green
            pepper and chives
Leaf lettuce, optional

In a large bowl, combine the gelatins; add boiling water and stir to dissolve. Drain pineapple, reserving the juice; set pineapple aside. Stir juice into gelatin. Refrigerate until slightly thickened. Stir in beets and pineapple. Pour into a 13-in. x 9-in. x 2-in. dish. Refrigerate until firm.

For dressing, combine the mayonnaise, sour cream, celery, green pepper and chives in a small bowl. Cut the gelatin into squares and serve on lettuce-lined salad plates if desired. Dollop squares with dressing. **Yield:** 12-15 servings.

Mushroom Broccoli Medley

This side dish has a wonderful blend of flavors. The colorful combination looks festive during the holidays.
—*Edie Draper, Pensacola Beach, Florida*

        6 bacon strips, cut into 1/2-inch pieces
        1 cup sliced fresh mushrooms
    1/2 cup chopped green onions
    1/4 cup chicken broth
    1/4 teaspoon salt, optional
    1/8 teaspoon pepper
        4 cups broccoli florets

In a skillet, cook bacon over medium heat until crisp. Remove to paper towels. Drain, reserving 2 tablespoons drippings. Saute mushrooms and onions in the drippings for 2-3 minutes or until tender. Add broth, salt if desired and pepper; bring to a boil. Reduce heat; simmer, uncovered, for 3-4 minutes.

Meanwhile, in a saucepan, bring broccoli and 1 in. of water to a boil. Reduce heat; cover and simmer for 3-5 minutes or until crisp-tender. Drain. Add broccoli and bacon to mushroom mixture; toss to coat. **Yield:** 6 servings.

Molasses Cutouts

Making these soft, chewy cookies with a rich flavor has been a family tradition since my children were small.
—*Sue Bartlett, Berlin, Wisconsin*

        1 cup butter (no substitutes), softened
        1 cup sugar
        2 eggs
        1 cup molasses
    1/2 cup cold water
    5-1/2 cups all-purpose flour
        4 teaspoons baking soda
        1 teaspoon salt
        1 teaspoon *each* ground cinnamon and ginger
FROSTING:
        4 cups confectioners' sugar
    1/4 cup butter, softened
        1 teaspoon ground ginger
    1/2 teaspoon salt
    1/2 teaspoon ground cinnamon
        3 to 4 tablespoons boiling water
M&M baking bits *or* other candies

In a mixing bowl, cream butter and sugar. Add eggs, one at a time, beating well after each. Beat in molasses and water. Combine flour, baking soda, salt, cinnamon and ginger; gradually add to creamed mixture. Cover and refrigerate 4 hours or until easy to handle.

On a lightly floured surface, roll out dough to 1/8-in. thickness. Cut with a 5-in. gingerbread man cutter. Place 1 in. apart on ungreased baking sheets. Bake at 375° for 6-8 minutes or until edges are golden brown. Remove to wire racks to cool.

For frosting, in a mixing bowl, combine confectioners' sugar, butter, ginger, salt, cinnamon and enough water to achieve spreading consistency. Frost and decorate cookies. **Yield:** about 3 dozen.

Classic Chili

Mom's chili was the best! She knew just the right ingredients to put her "stamp" on it. I could eat it with my eyes closed and know it was her recipe! It amazed me that she could put it together in so little time.
—Marjorie Carey, Belfry, Montana

1 medium green pepper, chopped
2 medium onions, chopped
1/2 cup chopped celery
1 tablespoon vegetable oil
2 pounds ground beef
2 cans (28 ounces *each*) diced tomatoes, undrained
1 can (8 ounces) tomato sauce
1 cup water
2 tablespoons Worcestershire sauce
1 to 2 tablespoons chili powder
1 teaspoon garlic powder
1 teaspoon dried oregano
1 teaspoon salt
1/2 teaspoon pepper
2 cans (16 ounces *each*) kidney beans, rinsed and drained

In a Dutch oven or large soup kettle, saute green pepper, onions and celery in oil until tender, about 5 minutes. Add ground beef and cook until browned; drain.

Stir in tomatoes, tomato sauce, water, Worcestershire sauce and seasonings. Bring to a boil; reduce heat. Cover and simmer for 1-1/2 hours, stirring occasionally. Add kidney beans. Simmer, uncovered, 10 minutes longer. **Yield:** 10-12 servings (3 quarts).

Cheddar Chive Bread

This bread is the perfect accompaniment to a piping-hot bowl of chili. In addition to a garnish of cheddar cheese on the chili, which Mom often added, we had her wonderful bread, chock-full of cheese flavor.
—Marjorie Carey

2 packages (1/4 ounce *each*) active dry yeast
2 cups warm water (110° to 115°)
5-3/4 to 6-1/4 cups all-purpose flour
3 cups (12 ounces) shredded cheddar cheese
1/2 cup chopped dried chives
1/4 cup butter *or* margarine, softened
1/4 cup sugar
1-1/2 teaspoons salt
1 teaspoon dried thyme

In a large mixing bowl, dissolve yeast in warm water. Add 3 cups flour, cheese, chives, butter, sugar, salt and thyme; beat for 2 minutes. Stir in enough of the remaining flour to form a soft dough.

Turn onto a floured surface; knead until smooth and elastic, about 6-8 minutes. Place in a greased bowl, turning once to grease top. Cover and let rise in a warm place until doubled, about 1 hour.

Punch dough down. Shape into two loaves and place in greased 9-in. x 5-in. x 3-in. loaf pans. Cover and let rise in a warm place until doubled, about 30 minutes. Bake at 350° for 40-45 minutes or until golden brown. Remove from pans to cool on a wire rack. **Yield:** 2 loaves.

Garden Olive Salad

We knew Mom had been shopping if we had this salad. The ingredients were always fresh. I can't remember one December Saturday that she didn't manage to serve our favorite salad.
—Marjorie Carey

1 medium head iceberg lettuce, torn
1 small onion, chopped
1 medium green pepper, chopped
2 cans (2-1/4 ounces *each*) sliced ripe olives, drained
4 medium tomatoes, cut into wedges
4 ounces Swiss cheese, cubed
Salad dressing of your choice

In a salad bowl, combine first six ingredients. Add dressing; toss. Serve immediately. **Yield:** 6-8 servings.

Easy Cranberry Pie

As a special treat when making this pie, Mom would sometimes place a marshmallow in the center of each lattice square, or, in honor of the Christmas tree we had just brought home, she'd cut Christmas tree shapes from the pie dough and place them on top of the pie.
—Marjorie Carey

2 cans (16 ounces *each*) whole-berry cranberry sauce
1/4 cup packed brown sugar
2 tablespoons butter *or* margarine, softened
Pastry for double-crust pie (9 inches)

In a bowl, combine cranberry sauce, brown sugar and butter. Line pie plate with bottom pastry; add filling. Top with a lattice crust. Bake at 350° for 50-60 minutes or until the crust is lightly browned. **Yield:** 6-8 servings.

Editor's Note: For a festively decorated pie, use a cookie cutter to cut out Christmas tree shapes from the top pastry instead of using a lattice crust. Place the dough shapes on an ungreased baking sheet and bake at 350° for 10-15 minutes or until golden. Cool slightly; arrange on top of baked pie.

Lively Leftovers

Leftover chili is great spooned over spaghetti or on a baked potato, or as a topping for hot dogs.

Creamed Turkey Over Rice

This is one of our favorite ways to have leftover turkey. When I buy a turkey for my family of five, I choose the largest one so we are sure to have plenty of leftovers. This recipe is simple to prepare and absolutely delicious.
—Kathi Parker, Hendersonville, North Carolina

    1 medium onion, chopped
1/2 cup chopped celery
1/4 cup butter *or* margarine
1/4 cup all-purpose flour
1-1/2 cups chicken broth
    2 cups cubed cooked turkey
    1 cup milk
1/2 cup cubed Swiss cheese
    1 tablespoon diced pimientos
1/2 teaspoon salt
1/4 teaspoon pepper
1/4 teaspoon ground nutmeg
Hot long grain and wild rice

In a skillet, saute onion and celery in butter until tender. Stir in flour until blended. Gradually stir in broth. Bring to a boil; boil and stir for 2 minutes.

    Reduce heat; stir in turkey, milk, cheese, pimientos, salt, pepper and nutmeg. Cook until cheese is melted and mixture is heated through. Serve over rice. **Yield:** 4 servings.

Special Scalloped Corn

The addition of carrots and green pepper makes this a colorful dish, which also grabs attention at a potluck. This casserole is also great when you need to prepare a dish ahead of time. All you need to do is bake it before serving.   *—Mrs. J. Brown, Fort Dodge, Iowa*

    1 can (14-3/4 ounces) cream-style corn
    2 eggs
1/2 cup crushed saltines (about 15 crackers)
1/4 cup butter *or* margarine, melted
1/4 cup evaporated milk
1/4 cup shredded carrot
1/4 cup chopped green pepper
    1 tablespoon chopped celery
    1 teaspoon chopped onion
1/2 teaspoon sugar
1/2 teaspoon salt
1/2 cup shredded cheddar cheese

In a bowl, combine the first 11 ingredients; mix well. Transfer to a greased 1-qt. baking dish. Sprinkle with cheese. Bake, uncovered, at 350° for 30-35 minutes or until a knife inserted near the center comes out clean. **Yield:** 4 servings.

Fruity Lime Salad Mold

A dear friend shared this recipe with me over 30 years ago, and it has appeared on our table frequently all these years. It's rich tasting, plus the touch of red maraschino cherries makes it a real treat for the holidays or any special occasion.   *—Jean Kirkland*
Newport, Oregon

    1 package (3 ounces) lime gelatin
    1 cup boiling water
    1 package (3 ounces) cream cheese, softened
    1 can (8 ounces) crushed pineapple,
       undrained
    1 cup heavy whipping cream, whipped
1/4 cup chopped pecans
1/4 cup chopped maraschino cherries

In a large bowl, dissolve gelatin in boiling water; chill until syrupy. In a small bowl, combine cream cheese and pineapple; stir into cooled gelatin. Fold in whipped cream, pecans and cherries.

    Pour into a 4-cup mold coated with nonstick cooking spray. Refrigerate for 3 hours or overnight. **Yield:** 6-8 servings.

Gingerbread with Brown Sugar Sauce

The aroma of gingerbread is what I remember most about my grandmother's kitchen, and it meant dessert would be special. That was nearly 50 years ago, but whenever I catch a whiff of ginger and cinnamon, I'm back with Grandmother and the happiness I knew.
—Toni Hamm, Vandergrift, Pennsylvania

    6 tablespoons shortening
1/2 cup packed brown sugar
1/3 cup molasses
    1 egg
1-1/2 cups all-purpose flour
1/2 teaspoon baking soda
1/2 teaspoon ground cinnamon
1/2 teaspoon ground ginger
1/8 teaspoon salt
1/2 cup buttermilk
BROWN SUGAR SAUCE:
    1 cup packed brown sugar
4-1/2 teaspoons cornstarch
1/2 cup cold water
1-1/2 teaspoons vinegar
    1 tablespoon butter *or* margarine
1-1/2 teaspoons vanilla extract

In a mixing bowl, cream shortening, brown sugar, molasses and egg; mix well. Combine flour, baking soda, cinnamon, ginger and salt; add to the molasses mixture alternately with buttermilk. Pour into a greased 9-in. round baking pan.

    Bake at 350° for 25-30 minutes or until a toothpick inserted near the center comes out clean. Cool for 10 minutes before removing from pan to a wire rack to cool completely.

    For sauce, combine brown sugar, cornstarch, water and vinegar in a saucepan; stir until smooth. Add butter. Bring to a boil; boil and stir for 2 minutes. Remove from the heat and stir in vanilla. Serve over the gingerbread. **Yield:** 6-8 servings.

Barbecued Pot Roast

When I was married over 45 years ago, my mother gave me this recipe. I always prepared this dish when we had company because it never failed and was so good! Through the years, it became one of my family's favorite meals. —Emma Nye, New Oxford, Pennsylvania

      2 teaspoons salt
  1/4 teaspoon pepper
      1 beef chuck roast (3 pounds)
      3 tablespoons vegetable oil
      1 can (8 ounces) tomato sauce
      1 cup water
      3 medium onions, sliced
      2 garlic cloves, minced
  1/4 cup lemon juice
  1/4 cup ketchup
      2 tablespoons brown sugar
      1 tablespoon Worcestershire sauce
  1/2 teaspoon ground mustard

Combine salt and pepper; rub over roast. Heat oil in a Dutch oven; brown roast on all sides. Add the tomato sauce, water, onions and garlic. Cover and simmer for 30 minutes.

Combine remaining ingredients; pour over meat. Cover and simmer for 3-4 hours or until the meat is tender. **Yield:** 6 servings.

Poppy Seed Cheese Bread

This easy-to-make bread goes well with a salad luncheon or a casserole dinner. But I especially like to serve it with spaghetti and pasta dishes. The cheese topping is its crowning glory! —Elaine Mundt, Detroit, Michigan

      1 package (1/4 ounce) active dry yeast
      2 teaspoons sugar
  1/4 cup warm water (110° to 115°)
  3/4 cup warm milk (110° to 115°)
      2 tablespoons shortening
      1 teaspoon salt
  2-1/4 to 2-1/2 cups all-purpose flour
  TOPPING:
      1 egg
      5 tablespoons milk
      1 teaspoon minced onion
      2 cups (8 ounces) shredded sharp cheddar
         cheese
  Poppy seeds

In a mixing bowl, dissolve the yeast and sugar in water. Combine milk, shortening and salt; stir into yeast mixture. Add enough flour to make a soft dough. Turn onto a floured surface; knead until smooth and elastic, about 3 minutes. Place in a greased bowl, turning once to grease top. Cover and let rise in a warm place until doubled, about 1-1/2 hours.

Punch the dough down; press into a greased 13-in. x 9-in. x 2-in. baking pan. Cover and let rise in a warm place until nearly doubled, about 45 minutes. Combine egg, milk, onion and cheese; spread over top of dough.

Sprinkle with poppy seeds. Bake at 425° for 15-20 minutes. Cut into squares; serve warm. **Yield:** 12-15 servings.

Tomato Crouton Casserole

Here's a side dish that's absolutely delicious. I've enjoyed making it for so many years that I don't recall where I got the recipe. This is a perfect accompaniment to most any entree because it's so attractive to serve and quick to prepare. —Dorothy Pritchett, Wills Point, Texas

      1 can (28 ounces) diced tomatoes, undrained
      2 cups seasoned stuffing croutons, *divided*
      1 small onion, chopped
      1 tablespoon sugar
  1/4 teaspoon dried oregano
  1/4 teaspoon salt
  1/8 teaspoon pepper
      3 tablespoons butter *or* margarine

In a greased 2-qt. baking dish, mix tomatoes and 1 cup croutons. Stir in onion, sugar, oregano, salt and pepper. Dot with butter; sprinkle with remaining croutons. Bake, uncovered, at 375° for 30-35 minutes. **Yield:** 6 servings.

Sour Cream Drops

My mother is an excellent baker, and this is her recipe. Whether Mom makes these cookies or I do, they always disappear quickly. Friends rave about them and often ask me to bring them to get-togethers. My young children enjoy all kinds of cookies, but these are their favorites. —Tracy Betzler, Reston, Virginia

  1/4 cup shortening
  3/4 cup sugar
      1 egg
  1/2 cup sour cream
  1/2 teaspoon vanilla extract
  1-1/3 cups all-purpose flour
  1/4 teaspoon baking soda
  1/4 teaspoon baking powder
  1/4 teaspoon salt
  BURNT SUGAR FROSTING:
      2 tablespoons butter *or* margarine
  1/2 cup confectioners' sugar
  1/4 teaspoon vanilla extract
      3 to 4 teaspoons hot water

In a mixing bowl, cream shortening, sugar and egg. Add sour cream and vanilla. Combine dry ingredients; add to the creamed mixture. Chill for at least 1 hour. Drop by tablespoonfuls 2 in. apart onto greased baking sheets. Bake at 425° for 7-8 minutes or until lightly browned. Remove to wire racks to cool.

For frosting, melt butter in a small saucepan until golden brown; stir in the sugar, vanilla and enough water to achieve a spreading consistency. Frost cooled cookies. **Yield:** about 2-1/2 dozen.

Turkey Apple Potpie

Years ago, a neighbor and I collaborated and submitted this recipe for an apple contest. We won first prize...a bushel of apples, of course. We had such fun experimenting, and I think of her whenever I make this dish. It's a favorite whenever I take it to a potluck or other group gathering.
—*Phyllis Atherton*
South Burlington, Vermont

1/4 cup chopped onion
1 tablespoon butter *or* margarine
2 cans (10-3/4 ounces *each*) condensed cream of chicken soup, undiluted
3 cups cubed cooked turkey
1 large tart apple, cubed
1/3 cup raisins
1 teaspoon lemon juice
1/4 teaspoon ground nutmeg
Pastry for single-crust pie (9 inches)

In a saucepan, saute onion in butter until tender. Add the soup, turkey, apple, raisins, lemon juice and nutmeg; mix well. Spoon into an ungreased 11-in. x 7-in. x 2-in. baking dish.

On a floured surface, roll pastry to fit top of dish. Cut vents in pastry, using a small apple cookie cutter if desired. Place over filling; flute edges. Bake at 425° for 25-30 minutes or until crust is golden brown and filling is bubbly. **Yield:** 6 servings.

Wild Rice and Squash Pilaf

The pilaf is fantastic with fish or poultry and especially compatible with turkey. Since it's so colorful, I like to think it makes my turkey "dressed for the holidays".
—*Erica Ollmann, San Diego, California*

1-1/2 cups sliced fresh mushrooms
1-1/2 cups diced peeled winter squash
2 medium onions, finely chopped
1/2 cup chopped green pepper
2 to 3 garlic cloves, minced
2 tablespoons olive *or* vegetable oil
3 cups cooked wild rice
1/2 cup chicken broth
1 tablespoon soy sauce
1/2 teaspoon dried savory
1/4 cup sliced almonds, toasted

In a large saucepan, saute mushrooms, squash, onions, green pepper and garlic in oil until crisp-tender, about 5-6 minutes. Stir in the rice. Add broth, soy sauce and savory. Cover and simmer for 13-15 minutes or until squash is tender. Toss with almonds if desired. **Yield:** 10 servings.

Cranberry Relish Salad

So much time and effort went into preparing meals for our large family that it was a real bonus to find a recipe with a shortcut. This salad was one of them. The dish became part of a special meal our family enjoyed during the holidays. I recall lots of second helpings being requested, but not many leftovers.
—*Rosemary Talcott, Worthington, Minnesota*

1 package (3 ounces) cherry gelatin
1 package (3 ounces) raspberry gelatin
1/4 cup sugar
1-1/2 cups boiling water
1 can (12 ounces) lemon-lime soda
1 can (8 ounces) crushed pineapple, undrained
2 packages (10 ounces *each*) frozen cranberry-orange sauce

In a large bowl, dissolve the gelatins and sugar in boiling water. Add the soda, pineapple and cranberry-orange sauce; chill until partially set. Pour into individual dishes or an 11-in. x 7-in. x 2-in. dish. Refrigerate overnight or until firm. **Yield:** 12 servings.

Soft Mincemeat Cookies

We call these "Santa's cookies" because they're what we put out for Santa instead of the usual decorated Christmas cutouts. These cookies remain a traditional part of my holiday baking. Besides a plate for Santa, they fill gift plates for family and friends. —*Evelyn Wadey Blackfalds, Alberta*

1/4 cup butter *or* margarine, softened
3/4 cup packed brown sugar
2 eggs
3/4 cup prepared mincemeat
1-1/2 cups all-purpose flour
1-1/2 teaspoons baking soda
1/2 teaspoon ground cinnamon
1/4 teaspoon ground nutmeg
1/4 teaspoon salt
1-1/2 cups (9 ounces) semisweet chocolate chips
1/2 cup chopped walnuts

In a mixing bowl, cream butter and brown sugar. Add eggs and mincemeat; mix well. Combine flour, baking soda, cinnamon, nutmeg and salt; add to creamed mixture. Mix well. Fold in chocolate chips and walnuts.

Drop by tablespoonfuls 2 in. apart onto greased baking sheets. Bake at 350° for 10-12 minutes or until golden brown. Cool on wire racks. **Yield:** about 4 dozen.

What Is Mincemeat?

Old-time mincemeat included ground meat in the mixture. Modern versions instead combine a combination of spicy chopped fruit. It is available in most grocery stores.

Lamb Chops with Prunes

Since I grow my own oranges, I often experiment by adding them to my favorite foods. I found this sweet fruit to be quite compatible with lamb, a meat I often serve. The wonderful orange juice-based sauce is simple to prepare, and its hint of spices really complements the lamb. —Margaret Pache, Mesa, Arizona

    8 loin lamb chops (1 inch thick)
    1 tablespoon vegetable oil
Salt and pepper to taste
    3/4 cup orange juice, *divided*
    2 tablespoons maple syrup
    1/2 teaspoon ground ginger
    1/4 teaspoon ground allspice
    8 ounces pitted prunes
1-1/2 teaspoons cornstarch

In a medium skillet, brown chops in oil on both sides; sprinkle with salt and pepper. Drain; return chops to skillet. Set aside 1 tablespoon of orange juice; pour remaining juice into skillet.

Add syrup, ginger and allspice; cover and cook over medium-low heat for 15 minutes, turning chops once. Add prunes. Cover and simmer until chops are tender.

Remove the chops to a serving platter and keep warm. Combine cornstarch and reserved orange juice; add to skillet. Bring to a boil over medium heat; cook and stir for 2 minutes. Spoon over lamb. **Yield:** 4 servings.

Blue-Ribbon Herb Rolls

These rolls have been a favorite of ours for nearly 25 years. The recipe won a blue ribbon at our county fair. —Mary Ann Evans, Tarpon Springs, Florida

    2 packages (1/4 ounce *each*) active dry yeast
2-3/4 cups warm water (110° to 115°), *divided*
    1 egg, beaten
    1/3 cup vegetable oil
    1/4 cup honey *or* molasses
    1 tablespoon salt
    2 teaspoons dill weed
    2 teaspoons dried thyme
    2 teaspoons dried basil
    1 teaspoon onion powder
    4 cups whole wheat flour
    4 to 4-1/2 cups all-purpose flour

In a mixing bowl, dissolve yeast in 1/2 cup warm water. Add next nine ingredients and remaining water; beat until smooth. Gradually add enough all-purpose flour to form a soft dough.

Turn onto a floured surface; knead until smooth and elastic, about 6-8 minutes. Place in a greased bowl, turning once to grease top. Cover and let rise in a warm place until doubled, about 1 hour.

Punch dough down. Shape into 1-in. balls. Place three balls each in greased muffin cups. Cover and let rise until doubled, 20-25 minutes. Bake at 375° for 12-15 minutes or until tops are golden brown. Remove from pan to a wire rack. **Yield:** 4 dozen.

Spinach Cheese Bake

Even those who aren't fond of spinach will find this dish very tasty, because the spinach flavor is mellowed by the cheese and eggs. —Elaine Hoehn, Merriam, Kansas

    3 tablespoons butter *or* margarine
    3 tablespoons all-purpose flour
1-1/2 cups milk
    2 cups (8 ounces) shredded process
      American cheese
    1 package (10 ounces) frozen chopped
      spinach, thawed and drained
1-1/2 cups soft bread crumbs
    3 eggs, lightly beaten
    1/2 teaspoon garlic salt
    1/4 teaspoon dried oregano
    1/4 teaspoon pepper

In a medium saucepan over low heat, melt butter; blend in flour until smooth. Cook and stir 1-2 minutes. Gradually stir in milk; bring to a boil. Cook and stir 2 minutes.

Remove from the heat; stir in cheese until melted. Add spinach, bread crumbs, eggs and seasonings; mix well. Spoon into an ungreased 1-1/2-qt. baking dish. Bake, uncovered, at 350° for 45-50 minutes or until lightly browned. **Yield:** 6-8 servings.

Chocolate Yum-Yum Cake

My grandmother first made this cake, and my mother made it often when I was a little girl. Today, I'm still baking it. What better testimony to a delicious recipe! —Dorothy Colli, West Hartford, Connecticut

    1/2 cup butter *or* margarine
    2 squares (1 ounce *each*) unsweetened baking
      chocolate
    1 cup sugar
    1/2 cup raisins
1-1/2 cups water
    1/2 teaspoon ground cinnamon
    1/4 teaspoon ground cloves
Pinch salt
1-1/2 teaspoons vanilla extract
1-3/4 cups all-purpose flour
    1 teaspoon baking soda
ICING:
    1/2 cup confectioners' sugar
    1/4 teaspoon vanilla extract
    1 to 2 teaspoons milk

In a large saucepan over low heat, melt butter and chocolate, stirring constantly. Add sugar, raisins, water, cinnamon and cloves; bring to a boil. Boil for 5 minutes, stirring occasionally. Remove from the heat; pour into a mixing bowl and cool for 15 minutes.

Add salt and vanilla. Combine flour and baking soda; add to chocolate mixture and mix well. Pour into a greased and floured 8-cup fluted tube pan. Bake at 350° for 45 minutes or until a toothpick inserted near the center comes out clean. Cool in pan for 10 minutes before removing to a wire rack to cool. Combine icing ingredients; spoon over cooled cake. **Yield:** 8-10 servings.

Golden Pancakes

My mother made these delicious pancakes for our family way back in the Depression years. She beat the batter by hand, but I use my blender to do the trick. It does a great job in breaking down the cottage cheese for a smooth batter.
—Ann Thomas
Telford, Pennsylvania

```
    6 eggs
    1 cup cream-style cottage cheese
1/2 cup all-purpose flour
1/4 cup milk
1/4 cup vegetable oil
1/2 teaspoon vanilla extract
1/4 teaspoon salt
```

In a blender, combine all ingredients. Cover and process on the highest speed for 1 minute.

Pour the batter by 1/4 cupfuls onto a greased hot griddle. Turn when bubbles form on top of pancakes; cook until the second side is golden brown. **Yield:** about 14 pancakes.

Onion Brunch Squares

I found this recipe years ago but have modified it to my family's liking. I make it with ham instead of bacon or without meat and have added various veggies to keep everyone happy. The recipe never fails and can be prepared ahead of time, so it's ideal for company .
—Danna Givot, San Diego, California

```
    2 large onions, chopped
    2 tablespoons butter or margarine
    1 tablespoon all-purpose flour
1/2 cup sour cream
1/2 teaspoon salt
1/2 teaspoon caraway seeds, optional
    3 eggs, lightly beaten
    3 bacon strips, cooked and crumbled
    1 tube (8 ounces) refrigerated crescent
      rolls
```

In a skillet, saute the onions in butter until tender; cool. Meanwhile, in a bowl, combine the flour, sour cream, salt and caraway seeds if desired until blended. Add the eggs and mix well. Stir in the bacon and reserved onions.

Unroll crescent roll dough into an ungreased 9-in. square baking pan. Press seams together to seal; press dough 1 in. up the sides of pan. Pour onion mixture into crust.

Bake at 375° for 25-30 minutes or until a knife inserted near the center comes out clean. **Yield:** 9 servings.

Saucy Fruit Medley

This is a variation of a recipe handed down from my mother-in-law. It can be used for brunch, as a refreshing dessert in summer or a colorful topping on yellow cake during the holidays. It keeps well in the refrigerator for a few days. This healthy combination can be stretched by adding more fruit and juice to the leftovers. The flavor improves each day.
—Linda Tucker
Farmington, Missouri

```
    1 can (21 ounces) cherry pie filling
    1 can (15 ounces) fruit cocktail, drained
    2 medium navel oranges, peeled and
      sectioned
    1 medium grapefruit, peeled and sectioned
    1 medium tart apple, peeled and diced
    1 cup strawberry-cranberry or raspberry-
      cranberry juice
1/2 cup chopped pecans, optional
```

In a large bowl, combine all ingredients. Cover and refrigerate for at least 1 hour before serving. **Yield:** 8-10 servings.

Danish Coffee Cake

My mother gave me this recipe when I was a teenager—it's something I treasure as a childhood memory. She made this tender, flaky pastry as part of a special breakfast on Sundays or holidays. I often bring these easy-to-fix pastries to ladies' meetings. They can't believe how good they taste with relatively few ingredients.
—Lee Deneau, Lansing, Michigan

```
    1 cup cold butter (no substitutes), divided
    2 cups all-purpose flour, divided
    2 tablespoons plus 1 cup water, divided
1/4 teaspoon salt
    3 eggs
ICING:
    2 tablespoons butter (no substitutes),
      softened
1-1/2 cups confectioners' sugar
1-1/2 teaspoons vanilla extract
    1 to 2 tablespoons water
1/2 cup chopped walnuts
```

In a bowl, cut 1/2 cup cold butter into 1 cup flour until mixture resembles coarse crumbs. Sprinkle with 2 tablespoons water; toss with a fork until mixture forms a ball. Divide into thirds. On a floured surface, roll each portion into a 9-in. x 6-in. rectangle. Place on greased baking sheets; set aside.

In a saucepan, bring salt and remaining butter and water to a boil. Add remaining flour all at once; stir until a smooth ball forms. Remove from the heat; let stand for 5 minutes. Add eggs, one at a time, beating well after each. Continue beating until mixture is smooth and shiny. Spread over the dough.

Bake at 400° for 30 minutes or until puffed and golden brown. Cool for 10 minutes before removing from pans to wire racks.

For icing, combine the butter, confectioners' sugar, vanilla extract and enough water to achieve the desired icing consistency. Spread over the warm coffee cakes. Sprinkle with walnuts. Store in the refrigerator. **Yield:** 3 coffee cakes.

Mother's Pasties

Everyone used to say my mom made the best pasties in the world. —Vivienne Abraham, Detroit, Michigan

    3 cups diced peeled potatoes
    1 cup diced carrots
    1 medium onion, chopped
  3/4 teaspoon salt
  1/4 teaspoon pepper
  1/2 pound ground beef
  1/4 pound ground pork
    1 tablespoon butter *or* margarine, melted
    4 cups all-purpose flour
1-1/4 teaspoons salt
    1 cup shortening
  3/4 cup cold water

In a bowl, combine the first five ingredients. Add beef and pork; mix well. Add butter and toss; set aside. For pastry, combine flour and salt in a bowl. Cut in shortening until the mixture resembles coarse crumbs. Gradually add water, tossing with a fork until a ball forms.

Divide into five portions; roll each into a 10-in. circle. Place 1 cup of filling in the center of each circle. Fold pastry over filling and seal edges tightly with a fork; cut slits in the top of each. Place on a greased baking sheet. Bake at 375° for 50-60 minutes or until golden brown. **Yield:** 5 servings.

Special Creamed Corn

This corn dish has a permanent place on our holiday table. My family loves it. —Deb Hauptmann Mohnton, Pennsylvania

  1/3 cup butter *or* margarine
  1/3 cup all-purpose flour
    1 cup heavy whipping cream
    1 cup milk
  1/4 cup sugar
    1 teaspoon salt
Dash white pepper
    5 cups frozen corn, thawed
  1/4 cup grated Parmesan cheese

In a saucepan, melt butter over medium heat. Stir in flour until smooth. Gradually add cream, milk, sugar, salt and pepper. Bring to a boil; boil and stir for 2 minutes. Add corn; heat through.

Transfer to an ungreased 1-1/2-qt. broiler-proof dish. Sprinkle with Parmesan cheese. Broil 5 in. from the heat for 3-5 minutes or until lightly browned and bubbly. **Yield:** 6-8 servings.

Bacon-Swiss Tossed Salad

This salad's pretty and tasty. Best of all, it can be put together before serving. When it's time, a simple toss and it's ready. —Cathee Bethel, Philomath, Oregon

  1/2 cup mayonnaise
    1 tablespoon sugar
  1/4 teaspoon *each* salt and pepper
    6 cups mixed salad greens
    1 medium red onion, sliced
    1 package (10 ounces) frozen peas, thawed
    8 ounces sliced Swiss cheese, julienned
    1 pound bacon, cooked and crumbled

In a bowl, combine mayonnaise, sugar, salt and pepper. In a salad bowl, layer a third of greens and a third of mayonnaise mixture, onion, peas and cheese. Repeat layers twice. Cover; refrigerate for 2 hours. Just before serving, add bacon; toss. **Yield:** 6-8 servings.

Raisin-Filled Torte

My mother used this recipe many times, and it was my favorite. She's gone now, but her memory lingers each time I bake it. —Jo Peapples, Brooksville, Florida

  1/2 cup shortening
1-1/4 cups sugar
    2 eggs
    2 cups cake flour
    2 teaspoons baking powder
  3/4 teaspoon salt
  3/4 cup milk
    1 teaspoon vanilla extract
1-1/2 teaspoons maple syrup
  1/4 teaspoon ground cinnamon
  1/8 teaspoon *each* ground cloves and nutmeg
FILLING:
  1/3 cup sugar
    1 tablespoon cornstarch
  2/3 cup water
1-1/2 cups raisins
    1 teaspoon lemon juice
    1 teaspoon butter *or* margarine
  1/4 teaspoon grated lemon peel
ICING:
    1 cup confectioners' sugar
    1 tablespoon butter *or* margarine, melted
  1/4 teaspoon grated lemon peel
    5 to 6 teaspoons milk

In a mixing bowl, cream shortening and sugar. Beat in eggs, one at a time. Combine flour, baking powder and salt; add to creamed mixture alternately with milk. Pour half of batter into another bowl. Add vanilla to one bowl; add syrup, cinnamon, cloves and nutmeg to second bowl. Pour each batter into a greased and floured 9-in. round cake pan. Bake at 375° for 20-25 minutes or until cakes test done. Cool for 10 minutes; remove from pans to wire racks to cool.

Combine sugar and cornstarch in a saucepan; stir in water until smooth. Add raisins. Bring to a boil; boil and stir for 2 minutes. Remove from the heat; stir in lemon juice, butter and peel. Cool.

In a small bowl, whisk sugar, butter and lemon peel. Add milk until icing reaches desired consistency. Place the spice cake layer on a serving platter; spread with filling. Top with vanilla cake layer and icing. **Yield:** 12 servings.

Baked Ham and Apples

When Mother wanted to serve ham, she went to the smokehouse, took one down from the rafters and sliced off as much as was needed. The rest was hung up again. This recipe is great if you use real smoked ham with no water added. When Mother prepared it this way, the flavor was especially sweet and buttery.
—Marjorie Schmidt, St. Marys, Ohio

    1 slice center-cut smoked ham (1 inch thick and 2 to 2-1/2 pounds)
    2 teaspoons ground mustard
    1/2 cup packed brown sugar
    3 medium tart apples
    2 tablespoons butter *or* margarine
Pepper to taste

Place ham in an ungreased 13-in. x 9-in. x 2-in. baking dish. Rub with mustard and sprinkle with brown sugar. Core apples and cut into 3/4-in. slices; arrange in a single layer over ham. Dot with butter and sprinkle with pepper.

Cover; bake at 400° for 15 minutes. Reduce heat to 325°; bake 45 minutes. Uncover; bake 15 minutes longer or until apples are tender. **Yield:** 6-8 servings.

Minty Peas and Onions

Mother could always rely on peas and onions when she was in a hurry and needed a quick side dish. Besides being easy to prepare, this dish was loved by everyone in our family. It was handed down to my mother by my grandmother. —Santa D'Addario, Brooklyn, New York

    2 large onions, cut into 1/2-inch wedges
    1/2 cup chopped sweet red pepper
    2 tablespoons vegetable oil
    2 packages (16 ounces *each*) frozen peas
    2 tablespoons minced fresh mint *or* 2 teaspoons dried mint

In a large skillet, saute onions and red pepper in oil until onions just begin to soften. Add peas; cook, uncovered, stirring occasionally, for 10 minutes or until heated through. Stir in mint and cook for 1 minute. **Yield:** 8 servings.

Skillet Herb Bread

My grandmother, aunts and mom were all good cooks, and each had her own specialty when it came to bread. But Mom's was my favorite.   *—Shirley Smith*
Yorba Linda, California

1-1/2 cups all-purpose flour
    2 tablespoons sugar
    4 teaspoons baking powder
1-1/2 teaspoons salt
    1 teaspoon rubbed sage
    1 teaspoon dried thyme
1-1/2 cups yellow cornmeal

1-1/2 cups chopped celery
    1 cup chopped onion
    1 jar (2 ounces) chopped pimientos, drained
    3 eggs, beaten
1-1/2 cups milk
    1/3 cup vegetable oil

In a large bowl, combine the flour, sugar, baking powder, salt, sage and thyme. Combine cornmeal, celery, onion and pimientos; add to dry ingredients and mix well. Add eggs, milk and oil; stir just until moistened.

Pour into a greased 10- or 11-in. ovenproof skillet. Bake at 400° for 35-45 minutes or until bread tests done. Serve warm. **Yield:** 10 servings.

Holiday Gumdrop Cookies

Making these cookies, I feel I'm keeping my mother's Christmas spirit alive. They were her special treat each year at holiday time. These cookies are great for keeping children busy—they can cut up the gumdrops and eat all the black ones (they turn the dough gray).
—Letah Chilston, Riverton, Wyoming

1-1/2 cups spice gumdrops
    3/4 cup coarsely chopped walnuts
    1/2 cup golden raisins
1-3/4 cups all-purpose flour, *divided*
    1 cup packed brown sugar
    1/2 cup shortening
    1 egg
    1/4 cup buttermilk
    1/2 teaspoon baking soda
    1/2 teaspoon salt

Cut the gumdrops into small pieces, reserving the black ones for another use. Place the remaining gumdrops in a bowl. Add walnuts, raisins and 1/4 cup flour; toss to coat. Set aside.

In a mixing bowl, cream brown sugar and shortening. Add egg; beat in buttermilk. Combine baking soda, salt and remaining flour; stir into creamed mixture. Add gumdrop mixture and mix well. Chill for 1 hour.

Drop by rounded teaspoonfuls 2 in. apart onto ungreased baking sheets. Bake at 400° for 8-10 minutes. Cool for 2 minutes before removing to a wire rack. **Yield:** about 3 dozen.

Freezing Holiday Cookies

Begin your cookie baking before Christmas. To freeeze cookies for up to 3 months, wrap the cookies in plastic, stack in an airtight container, seal and freeze. Thaw wrapped cookies at room temperature before serving.

Cranberry Meatballs

This is a versatile recipe to be used either as a main dish or as an appetizer. You simply adjust the size of the meatballs. One-inch meatballs are great as appetizers; make them 1-1/4 inches for a meal. I like to serve them during the holidays as an appetizer. It works well to curb appetites while your guests await the main meal.
—*Frances Venator, Ottumwa, Iowa*

    2 eggs, lightly beaten
    1 cup crushed saltines (about 15 crackers)
    1 medium onion, finely chopped
    2 teaspoons salt
  1/4 teaspoon pepper
    1 pound ground beef
    1 pound ground pork
    2 cans (16 ounces *each*) whole-berry
       cranberry sauce
    2 cans (10-3/4 ounces *each*) condensed
       tomato soup, undiluted
    1 teaspoon prepared mustard

In a bowl, combine the first five ingredients; add beef and pork and mix well. Shape into 1-in. meatballs. Place on a rack in a 15-in. x 10-in. x 1-in. baking pan. Bake at 400° for 15 minutes.

Meanwhile, combine the cranberry sauce, soup and mustard in a large saucepan. Bring to a boil. Reduce heat; add the meatballs. Simmer, uncovered, for 10 minutes. **Yield:** 5 dozen.

Editor's Note: To serve the meatballs as a main dish instead of an appetizer, make 1-1/4-inch balls and bake for 20 minutes.

Zippy Cheese Dip

I first tasted this cheese dip in a cooking class I took at a local supermarket. We learned that it isn't necessary to add the eggs, but they give the dip a thicker consistency. It is scrumptious served with a variety of crackers.
—*Diane Hixon*
Niceville, Florida

  1/4 cup chopped onion
    1 tablespoon butter *or* margarine
    1 can (14-1/2 ounces) diced tomatoes,
       drained
    1 pound process American cheese, cubed
    1 teaspoon Worcestershire sauce
  1/2 teaspoon paprika
  1/4 teaspoon salt
    2 drops hot pepper sauce
    2 eggs, beaten
Assorted crackers

In a saucepan, saute the onion in butter until tender. Add the tomatoes, American cheese, Worcestershire sauce, paprika, salt and hot pepper sauce. Cook and stir over medium heat until the cheese is melted. Remove from the heat.

Stir a small amount of hot mixture into eggs. Return all to the pan, stirring constantly. Cook and stir until mixture reaches 160°. Serve warm with crackers. Store leftovers in the refrigerator. **Yield:** 3-1/2 cups.

Rosy Fruit Punch

This recipe goes a long way to satisfy the thirst of your guests. All the flavors of the holiday season are in this colorful and refreshing punch. —*Joyce Brown*
Genesee, Idaho

    1 bottle (128 ounces) cranberry juice, chilled
    1 carton (64 ounces) orange juice, chilled
    6 cups cold water
    3 cups pineapple juice, chilled
    3 cups sugar
  3/4 cup lemon juice

In a large punch bowl, combine all ingredients; stir until sugar is dissolved. **Yield:** about 8-1/2 quarts.

Ham Salad Spread

My family has enjoyed this hearty ham salad spread for years. It came to be an expected leftover every time we had ham for a special dinner. Recently, I decided to measure the ingredients, write down the recipe and pass it on to my daughter and daughter-in-law.
—*Marcella Kulp, Quakertown, Pennsylvania*

    3 cups ground fully cooked ham
    1 hard-cooked egg, chopped
    2 tablespoons finely chopped celery
    2 teaspoons finely chopped onion
    2 teaspoons sweet pickle relish
  3/4 cup mayonnaise
    1 tablespoon prepared mustard
Assorted crackers

In a bowl, combine the first five ingredients. Combine mayonnaise and mustard; add to ham mixture and mix well. Refrigerate until serving. Serve with crackers. **Yield:** 3 cups.

Planning a Party

For a large gathering of family and friends, have a buffet. It's more flexible than a sit-down meal, doesn't require serving, and lets you offer a wider variety of food to please different tastes.

When setting up a buffet, keep drinks on a separate table from the food. Arrange the food table with plates at the start, side dishes and main courses in the middle, and silverware and napkins at the end.

How much food do you need for a large gathering? Figure on 1/2 pound of meat per person, 1/2 to 1 cup each of starches and vegetables and 1 cup of salad. For pre-meal nibbles, plan on eight hors d'oeuvres a person each hour.

General Recipe Index

A

APPETIZERS
Crabby Deviled Eggs, 39
Ham Salad Spread, 107
Zippy Cheese Dip, 107

APPLES
Apple Iceberg Salad, 39
Apple Mashed Potatoes, 85
Apple Walnut Squares, 69
Baked Ham and Apples, 105
Cinnamon Apple Salad, 73
Grandma's Apples and Rice, 75
Pork Roast with Spiced Apples, 21
Turkey Apple Potpie, 97

ASPARAGUS
Asparagus Supreme, 11
Creamy Asparagus Casserole, 7

B

BANANAS
Banana Cream Dessert, 53
Bananas 'n' Cream Bundt Cake, 21

BARS
Apple Walnut Squares, 69
Date Bar Dessert, 39
Lemon Bars, 47
Lemon Graham Squares, 37
Pineapple Cheesecake Squares, 11

BEANS
Green Beans with Cherry Tomatoes, 33
Green Beans with Zucchini, 67
Marjoram Green Beans, 85
Old-Fashioned Baked Beans, 45
Peppered Green Beans, 77
Squash Rings with Green Beans, 81
Sweet-and-Sour Green Beans, 21

BEEF & CORNED BEEF (also see
Ground Beef)
Autumn Vegetable Beef Stew, 59
Barbecued Pot Roast, 95
Barbecued Round Steak, 69
Beef Rouladen, 87
Braised Beef Rolls, 9
Corned Beef and Cabbage, 13
Deviled Corned Beef Buns, 53
Old-Fashioned Swiss Steak, 43
Sauerbraten, 79
Spiced Pot Roast, 75
Steak Over Potatoes, 29

BEETS
Beet Relish, 13
Ruby-Red Beet Salad, 89

BEVERAGES
Fruit Cooler, 27
Rosy Fruit Punch, 107

BISCUITS
Baking Powder Biscuits, 75
Feather-Light Biscuits, 43

BREADS (also see Biscuits; Doughnuts
& Pastry; Rolls; Yeast Breads)
Irish Soda Bread, 13
Pull-Apart Herb Bread, 65
Pumpkin Bread Ring, 67
Skillet Herb Bread, 105

BROCCOLI
Creamy Broccoli Casserole, 61
Mushroom Broccoli Medley, 89
Raisin Broccoli Salad, 37
Zesty Broccoli, 41

BRUSSELS SPROUTS
Bacon-Topped Brussels Sprouts, 87
Special Brussels Sprouts, 9

C

CABBAGE
Basil Dill Coleslaw, 19
Corned Beef and Cabbage, 13
Creamy Coleslaw, 53
Favorite Cabbage Salad, 69
Sweet-and-Sour Red Cabbage, 79

CAKES & CUPCAKES
Bananas 'n' Cream Bundt Cake, 21
Chocolate Yum-Yum Cake, 99
Choco-Scotch Marble Cake, 85
Emerald Isle Cake, 13
Gingerbread with Brown Sugar Sauce, 93
Maple Carrot Cupcakes, 33
Orange Chiffon Cake, 27
Orange Zucchini Cake, 55
Raisin-Filled Torte, 103

CARROTS
Baked Carrots, 43
Buttery Carrots 'n' Onions, 29
Maple Carrot Cupcakes, 33

CASSEROLES
Main Dishes
   Ham 'n' Egg Casserole, 23

   Spanish Corn with Fish Sticks, 37
Side Dishes
   Asparagus Supreme, 11
   Cheddar Mushroom Macaroni, 19
   Creamy Asparagus Casserole, 7
   Creamy Broccoli Casserole, 61
   Louisiana Sweet Potato Casserole, 77
   Macaroni Au Gratin, 15
   Mother's Manicotti, 25
   Scalloped Cheese Potatoes, 49
   Special Creamed Corn, 103
   Special Scalloped Corn, 93
   Spinach Cheese Bake, 99
   Spinach Pecan Bake, 63
   Sweet Potato Casserole, 67
   Tomato Crouton Casserole, 95
   Turnip Souffle, 75

CHEESE
Bacon-Swiss Tossed Salad, 103
Berry Cheesecake Parfaits, 77
Blue Cheese Salad, 17
Cheddar Chive Bread, 91
Cheddar Mushroom Macaroni, 19
Easter Pie, 25
Macaroni Au Gratin, 15
Mother's Manicotti, 25
Parmesan Noodles, 65
Pineapple Cheesecake Squares, 11
Poppy Seed Cheese Bread, 95
Scalloped Cheese Potatoes, 49
Spinach Cheese Bake, 99
Stovetop Macaroni and Cheese, 71
Zippy Cheese Dip, 107

CHERRIES
George Washington Cherry Cobbler, 9
Ham Cups with Cherry Sauce, 15
Slow-Cooked Cherry Pork Chops, 85

CHICKEN
Arizona Chicken, 55
Baked Lemon Chicken, 33
Butter Roast Chicken, 11
Chicken with Peach Stuffing, 81
Cider-Roasted Chicken, 73
Crispy Lemon-Fried Chicken, 51
Deep-Dish Chicken Potpie, 27
Oven Chicken Stew, 67
Slow-Cooked Orange Chicken, 41

CHOCOLATE
Chocolate Yum-Yum Cake, 99
Choco-Scotch Marble Cake, 85
White Chocolate Chip Hazelnut
   Cookies, 19

COBBLERS
Country Plum Crumble, 59
George Washington Cherry Cobbler, 9
Zucchini Cobbler, 45

COLESLAW
Basil Dill Coleslaw, 19
Creamy Coleslaw, 53

COOKIES *(also see Bars)*
Chewy Ginger Drop Cookies, 63
Crisp Lemon Sugar Cookies, 29
Holiday Gumdrop Cookies, 105
Molasses Cutouts, 89
Soft Mincemeat Cookies, 97
Sour Cream Drops, 95
White Chocolate Chip Hazelnut
    Cookies, 19

CORN
Spanish Corn with Fish Sticks, 37
Special Creamed Corn, 103
Special Scalloped Corn, 93

CORN BREAD & CORNMEAL
Chili Cornmeal Crescents, 55
Cornmeal Pie, 71
Turkey with Corn-Bread Dressing, 61

CRANBERRIES
Cranberry Meatballs, 107
Cranberry Relish Salad, 97
Easy Cranberry Pie, 91

CUCUMBERS
Cool Cucumber Salad, 11
Pennsylvania Dutch Cucumbers, 51

DESSERTS *(also see specific kinds)*
Baked Lemon Pudding, 17
Banana Cream Dessert, 53
Berry Cheesecake Parfaits, 77
Coffee Ice Cream, 35
Peach Kuchen, 79
Pumpkin Custard, 73
Rhubarb Peach Shortcake, 15
Strawberry Schaum Torte, 87
Strawberry Shortcake, 51

DOUGHNUTS & PASTRY
Blue-Ribbon Doughnuts, 23
Danish Coffee Cake, 101

EGGS
Crabby Deviled Eggs, 39
Ham 'n' Egg Casserole, 23
Onion Brunch Squares, 101

FISH & SEAFOOD
Broiled Fish, 17
Crabby Deviled Eggs, 39
New England Salmon Pie, 89
Pan-Fried Trout, 47
Salmon Cakes, 71
Spanish Corn with Fish Sticks, 37

FRUIT *(also see specific kinds)*
Apricot Salad, 61
Berry Cheesecake Parfaits, 77
Country Plum Crumble, 59
Creamy Fruit Bowl, 23
Fresh Fruit Medley, 33
Fruit Cooler, 27
Ginger Pear Gelatin, 27
Greens 'n' Grapefruit Salad, 87
Pudding-Topped Fruit Salad, 37
Rosy Fruit Punch, 107
Saucy Fruit Medley, 101
Spring Fruit Salad, 7

GROUND BEEF
Classic Chili, 91
Cranberry Meatballs, 107
Deluxe Bacon Burgers, 35
Mother's Pasties, 103
Poor Man's Steak, 49
Sicilian Meat Roll, 65
Tasty Sloppy Joes, 19

HAM & BACON
Bacon-Swiss Tossed Salad, 103
Bacon-Topped Brussels Sprouts, 87
Baked Ham and Apples, 105
Chef's Salad, 43
Deluxe Bacon Burgers, 35
Ham 'n' Egg Casserole, 23
Ham Cups with Cherry Sauce, 15
Ham Salad Spread, 107
Mustard-Glazed Ham, 7

L
LAMB
Lamb Chops with Prunes, 99
Leg of Lamb, 25

LEMON & LIME
Baked Lemon Chicken, 33
Baked Lemon Pudding, 17
Crisp Lemon Sugar Cookies, 29
Crispy Lemon-Fried Chicken, 51
Fruity Lime Salad Mold, 93
Lemon Bars, 47
Lemon Graham Squares, 37
Lemony Marinated Vegetables, 59

M
MEAT LOAVES & MEATBALLS
Cranberry Meatballs, 107
Ham Cups with Cherry Sauce, 15
Sicilian Meat Roll, 65
Stuffed Turkey Roll, 77

MEAT PIES
Deep-Dish Chicken Potpie, 27
Mother's Pasties, 103
New England Salmon Pie, 89
Turkey Apple Potpie, 97

MUSHROOMS
Cheddar Mushroom Macaroni, 19
Cream of Mushroom Soup, 9
Mushroom Broccoli Medley, 89

N
NUTS & PEANUT BUTTER
Apple Walnut Squares, 69
Peanutty Pie, 49
Spinach Pecan Bake, 63
White Chocolate Chip Hazelnut
    Cookies, 19

O
ONIONS & CHIVES
Buttery Carrots 'n' Onions, 29
Cheddar Chive Bread, 91
Minty Peas and Onions, 105
Onion Brunch Squares, 101
Onion Pie, 63

ORANGE
Orange Buttermilk Salad, 15
Orange Chiffon Cake, 27
Orange Meringue Pie, 81
Orange Zucchini Cake, 55
Slow-Cooked Orange Chicken, 41

OVEN ENTREES *(also see
Casseroles; Meat Loaves & Meatballs;
Meat Pies)*
Baked Ham and Apples, 105
Baked Lemon Chicken, 33
Braised Beef Rolls, 9
Broiled Fish, 17
Butter Roast Chicken, 11
Cider-Roasted Chicken, 73
Leg of Lamb, 25
Mustard-Glazed Ham, 7
Old-Fashioned Swiss Steak, 43
Oven-Barbecued Spareribs, 45
Poor Man's Steak, 49
Pork Roast with Spiced Apples, 21
Spiced Pot Roast, 75
Steak Over Potatoes, 29
Turkey with Corn-Bread Dressing, 61

P

PANCAKES
Golden Pancakes, 101
Old-World Puff Pancake, 23

PASTA & NOODLES
Cheddar Mushroom Macaroni, 19
Macaroni Au Gratin, 15
Mother's Manicotti, 25
Parmesan Noodles, 65
Stovetop Macaroni and Cheese, 71

PEACHES
Chicken with Peach Stuffing, 81
Peach Kuchen, 79
Rhubarb Peach Shortcake, 15

PEAS
Creamed Peas, 71
Creamed Sweet Peas, 47
Minty Peas and Onions, 105

PEPPERS
Peppered Green Beans, 77
Salad with Tomato-Green Pepper
    Dressing, 29

PIES
Cornmeal Pie, 71
Easter Pie, 25
Easy Cranberry Pie, 91
Harvest Sweet Potato Pie, 61
Orange Meringue Pie, 81
Peanutty Pie, 49
Pineapple Coconut Pie, 41

PINEAPPLE
Pineapple Cheesecake Squares, 11
Pineapple Coconut Pie, 41

PORK *(also see Ham & Bacon)*
Cranberry Meatballs, 107
Herbed Pork Roast, 63
Mother's Pasties, 103
Oven-Barbecued Spareribs, 45
Pork Roast with Spiced Apples, 21
Slow-Cooked Cherry Pork Chops, 85
Tangy Pork Barbecue, 39

POTATOES & SWEET POTATOES
Apple Mashed Potatoes, 85
Harvest Sweet Potato Pie, 61
Homemade Potato Salad, 35
Louisiana Sweet Potato Casserole, 77
Potato Dumplings, 79
Potato Rolls, 7
Red Potato Salad, 51
Roasted New Potatoes, 17
Scalloped Cheese Potatoes, 49
Steak Over Potatoes, 29
Sweet Potato Casserole, 67

PUMPKIN
Pumpkin Bread Ring, 67
Pumpkin Custard, 73

R

RAISINS & DATES
Date Bar Dessert, 39
Irish Soda Bread, 13
Raisin Broccoli Salad, 37
Raisin-Filled Torte, 103

RICE
Baked Calico Rice, 69
Creamed Turkey Over Rice, 93
Grandma's Apples and Rice, 75
Vegetable Rice Medley, 55
Wild Rice and Squash Pilaf, 97

ROLLS
Blue-Ribbon Herb Rolls, 99
Chili Cornmeal Crescents, 55
Crusty Rolls, 59
Potato Rolls, 7
Spoon Rolls, 21

S

SALADS & DRESSINGS *(also see
Coleslaw)*
Dressing
    Mustard Salad Dressing, 81
Fruit and Gelatin Salads
    Apricot Salad, 61
    Cinnamon Apple Salad, 73
    Cool Cucumber Salad, 11
    Cranberry Relish Salad, 97
    Creamy Fruit Bowl, 23
    Fresh Fruit Medley, 33
    Fruity Lime Salad Mold, 93
    Ginger Pear Gelatin, 27
    Orange Buttermilk Salad, 15
    Pudding-Topped Fruit Salad, 37
    Ruby-Red Beet Salad, 89
    Saucy Fruit Medley, 101
    Spring Fruit Salad, 7
Green Salads
    Apple Iceberg Salad, 39
    Bacon-Swiss Tossed Salad, 103
    Blue Cheese Salad, 17
    Chef's Salad, 43
    Garden Olive Salad, 91
    Greens 'n' Grapefruit Salad, 87
    Mixed Greens Salad, 25
    Salad with Creamy Dressing, 45
    Salad with Tomato-Green Pepper
        Dressing, 29
    Three-Step Salad, 65
    12-Hour Salad, 49
Potato Salads
    Homemade Potato Salad, 35
    Red Potato Salad, 51
Vegetable Salads
    Colorful Vegetable Salad, 35

Favorite Cabbage Salad, 69
Lemony Marinated Vegetables, 59
Pennsylvania Dutch Cucumbers, 51
Raisin Broccoli Salad, 37
Summer Vegetable Salad, 53

SANDWICHES
Deluxe Bacon Burgers, 35
Deviled Corned Beef Buns, 53
Tangy Pork Barbecue, 39
Tasty Sloppy Joes, 19

SIDE DISHES *(also see Casseroles)*
Apple Mashed Potatoes, 85
Bacon-Topped Brussels Sprouts, 87
Baked Calico Rice, 69
Baked Carrots, 43
Beet Relish, 13
Buttery Carrots 'n' Onions, 29
Creamed Peas, 71
Creamed Sweet Peas, 47
Grandma's Apples and Rice, 75
Green Beans with Cherry Tomatoes, 33
Green Beans with Zucchini, 67
Marjoram Green Beans, 85
Minty Peas and Onions, 105
Mushroom Broccoli Medley, 89
Old-Fashioned Baked Beans, 45
Onion Pie, 63
Parmesan Noodles, 65
Peppered Green Beans, 77
Potato Dumplings, 79
Roasted New Potatoes, 17
Special Brussels Sprouts, 9
Squash Rings with Green Beans, 81
Stovetop Macaroni and Cheese, 71
Sweet-and-Sour Green Beans, 21
Sweet-and-Sour Red Cabbage, 79
Vegetable Rice Medley, 55
Wild Rice and Squash Pilaf, 97
Zesty Broccoli, 41

**SKILLET & STOVETOP
SUPPERS**
Arizona Chicken, 55
Barbecued Pot Roast, 95
Barbecued Round Steak, 69
Beef Rouladen, 87
Chicken with Peach Stuffing, 81
Corned Beef and Cabbage, 13
Creamed Turkey Over Rice, 93
Crispy Lemon-Fried Chicken, 51
Herbed Pork Roast, 63
Lamb Chops with Prunes, 99
Pan-Fried Trout, 47
Salmon Cakes, 71
Sauerbraten, 79

SLOW COOKER RECIPES
Slow-Cooked Cherry Pork Chops, 85
Slow-Cooked Orange Chicken, 41

SOUPS & CHILI
Butternut Squash Bisque, 73
Classic Chili, 91
Cream of Mushroom Soup, 9

SPINACH
Spinach Cheese Bake, 99
Spinach Pecan Bake, 63

SQUASH & ZUCCHINI
Butternut Squash Bisque, 73
Green Beans with Zucchini, 67
Orange Zucchini Cake, 55
Squash Rings with Green Beans, 81
Wild Rice and Squash Pilaf, 97
Zucchini Cobbler, 45

STEWS
Autumn Vegetable Beef Stew, 59

Oven Chicken Stew, 67

STRAWBERRIES
Strawberry Schaum Torte, 87
Strawberry Shortcake, 51

T
TOMATOES
Green Beans with Cherry Tomatoes, 33
Salad with Tomato-Green Pepper
    Dressing, 29
Tomato Crouton Casserole, 95

TURKEY
Creamed Turkey Over Rice, 93
Stuffed Turkey Roll, 77
Turkey Apple Potpie, 97
Turkey with Corn-Bread Dressing, 61

V
VEGETABLES (also see specific kinds)
Autumn Vegetable Beef Stew, 59
Colorful Vegetable Salad, 35
Garden Olive Salad, 91
Lemony Marinated Vegetables, 59
Summer Vegetable Salad, 53
Turnip Souffle, 75
Vegetable Rice Medley, 55

Y
YEAST BREADS (also see Rolls)
Caraway Rye Bread, 47
Cheddar Chive Bread, 91
Oatmeal Yeast Bread, 41
Poppy Seed Cheese Bread, 95

Alphabetical Index

A
Apple Iceberg Salad, 39
Apple Mashed Potatoes, 85
Apple Walnut Squares, 69
Apricot Salad, 61
Arizona Chicken, 55
Asparagus Supreme, 11
Autumn Vegetable Beef Stew, 59

B
Bacon-Swiss Tossed Salad, 103
Bacon-Topped Brussels Sprouts, 87
Baked Calico Rice, 69
Baked Carrots, 43
Baked Ham and Apples, 105
Baked Lemon Chicken, 33
Baked Lemon Pudding, 17
Baking Powder Biscuits, 75
Banana Cream Dessert, 53
Bananas 'n' Cream Bundt Cake, 21
Barbecued Pot Roast, 95
Barbecued Round Steak, 69
Basil Dill Coleslaw, 19
Beef Rouladen, 87
Beet Relish, 13
Berry Cheesecake Parfaits, 77
Blue Cheese Salad, 17
Blue-Ribbon Doughnuts, 23

Blue-Ribbon Herb Rolls, 99
Braised Beef Rolls, 9
Broiled Fish, 17
Butter Roast Chicken, 11
Butternut Squash Bisque, 73
Buttery Carrots 'n' Onions, 29

C
Caraway Rye Bread, 47
Cheddar Chive Bread, 91
Cheddar Mushroom Macaroni, 19
Chef's Salad, 43
Chewy Ginger Drop Cookies, 63
Chicken with Peach Stuffing, 81
Chili Cornmeal Crescents, 55
Chocolate Yum-Yum Cake, 99
Choco-Scotch Marble Cake, 85
Cider-Roasted Chicken, 73
Cinnamon Apple Salad, 73
Classic Chili, 91
Coffee Ice Cream, 35
Colorful Vegetable Salad, 35
Cool Cucumber Salad, 11
Corned Beef and Cabbage, 13
Cornmeal Pie, 71
Country Plum Crumble, 59
Crabby Deviled Eggs, 39
Cranberry Meatballs, 107

Cranberry Relish Salad, 97
Cream of Mushroom Soup, 9
Creamed Peas, 71
Creamed Sweet Peas, 47
Creamed Turkey Over Rice, 93
Creamy Asparagus Casserole, 7
Creamy Broccoli Casserole, 61
Creamy Coleslaw, 53
Creamy Fruit Bowl, 23
Crisp Lemon Sugar Cookies, 29
Crispy Lemon-Fried Chicken, 51
Crusty Rolls, 59

D
Danish Coffee Cake, 101
Date Bar Dessert, 39
Deep-Dish Chicken Potpie, 27
Deluxe Bacon Burgers, 35
Deviled Corned Beef Buns, 53

E
Easter Pie, 25
Easy Cranberry Pie, 91
Emerald Isle Cake, 13

F
Favorite Cabbage Salad, 69
Feather-Light Biscuits, 43

Fresh Fruit Medley, 33
Fruit Cooler, 27
Fruity Lime Salad Mold, 93

G

Garden Olive Salad, 91
George Washington Cherry Cobbler, 9
Ginger Pear Gelatin, 27
Gingerbread with Brown Sugar Sauce, 93
Golden Pancakes, 101
Grandma's Apples and Rice, 75
Green Beans with Cherry Tomatoes, 33
Green Beans with Zucchini, 67
Greens 'n' Grapefruit Salad, 87

H

Ham 'n' Egg Casserole, 23
Ham Cups with Cherry Sauce, 15
Ham Salad Spread, 107
Harvest Sweet Potato Pie, 61
Herbed Pork Roast, 63
Holiday Gumdrop Cookies, 105
Homemade Potato Salad, 35

I

Irish Soda Bread, 13

L

Lamb Chops with Prunes, 99
Leg of Lamb, 25
Lemon Bars, 47
Lemon Graham Squares, 37
Lemony Marinated Vegetables, 59
Louisiana Sweet Potato Casserole, 77

M

Macaroni Au Gratin, 15
Maple Carrot Cupcakes, 33
Marjoram Green Beans, 85
Minty Peas and Onions, 105
Mixed Greens Salad, 25
Molasses Cutouts, 89
Mother's Manicotti, 25
Mother's Pasties, 103
Mushroom Broccoli Medley, 89
Mustard-Glazed Ham, 7
Mustard Salad Dressing, 81

N

New England Salmon Pie, 89

O

Oatmeal Yeast Bread, 41
Old-Fashioned Baked Beans, 45
Old-Fashioned Swiss Steak, 43
Old-World Puff Pancake, 23
Onion Brunch Squares, 101
Onion Pie, 63
Orange Buttermilk Salad, 15
Orange Chiffon Cake, 27
Orange Meringue Pie, 81
Orange Zucchini Cake, 55
Oven-Barbecued Spareribs, 45
Oven Chicken Stew, 67

P

Pan-Fried Trout, 47
Parmesan Noodles, 65
Peach Kuchen, 79
Peanutty Pie, 49
Pennsylvania Dutch Cucumbers, 51
Peppered Green Beans, 77
Pineapple Cheesecake Squares, 11
Pineapple Coconut Pie, 41
Poor Man's Steak, 49
Poppy Seed Cheese Bread, 95
Pork Roast with Spiced Apples, 21
Potato Dumplings, 79
Potato Rolls, 7
Pudding-Topped Fruit Salad, 37
Pull-Apart Herb Bread, 65
Pumpkin Bread Ring, 67
Pumpkin Custard, 73

R

Raisin Broccoli Salad, 37
Raisin-Filled Torte, 103
Red Potato Salad, 51
Rhubarb Peach Shortcake, 15
Roasted New Potatoes, 17
Rosy Fruit Punch, 107
Ruby-Red Beet Salad, 89

S

Salad with Creamy Dressing, 45
Salad with Tomato-Green Pepper
    Dressing, 29

Salmon Cakes, 71
Saucy Fruit Medley, 101
Sauerbraten, 79
Scalloped Cheese Potatoes, 49
Sicilian Meat Roll, 65
Skillet Herb Bread, 105
Slow-Cooked Cherry Pork Chops, 85
Slow-Cooked Orange Chicken, 41
Soft Mincemeat Cookies, 97
Sour Cream Drops, 95
Spanish Corn with Fish Sticks, 37
Special Brussels Sprouts, 9
Special Creamed Corn, 103
Special Scalloped Corn, 93
Spiced Pot Roast, 75
Spinach Cheese Bake, 99
Spinach Pecan Bake, 63
Spoon Rolls, 21
Spring Fruit Salad, 7
Squash Rings with Green Beans, 81
Steak Over Potatoes, 29
Stovetop Macaroni and Cheese, 71
Strawberry Schaum Torte, 87
Strawberry Shortcake, 51
Stuffed Turkey Roll, 77
Summer Vegetable Salad, 53
Sweet-and-Sour Green Beans, 21
Sweet-and-Sour Red Cabbage, 79
Sweet Potato Casserole, 67

T

Tangy Pork Barbecue, 39
Tasty Sloppy Joes, 19
Three-Step Salad, 65
Tomato Crouton Casserole, 95
Turkey Apple Potpie, 97
Turkey with Corn-Bread Dressing, 61
Turnip Souffle, 75
12-Hour Salad, 49

U

Vegetable Rice Medley, 55
White Chocolate Chip Hazelnut
    Cookies, 19
Wild Rice and Squash Pilaf, 97

Z

Zesty Broccoli, 41
Zippy Cheese Dip, 107
Zucchini Cobbler, 45